MAKING DECORATIVE SCREENS

MAKING DECORATIVE SCREENS

Amanda Howes

GUILD OF MASTER CRAFTSMAN PUBLICATIONS LTD

First published 2000 by

Guild of Master Craftsman Publications Ltd

166 High Street, Lewes,

East Sussex BN7 1XU

Reprinted 2001

Finished item photography by Chris Skarbon;
other photographs by Amanda Howes

Styling by Helena Furness

Illustrations by John Yates

ISBN 1 86108 142 1

Designed by Fran Rawlinson

Typeface: Helvetica and Bodoni

Colour origination by Viscan Graphics (Singapore)

Printed and bound by Kyodo Printing (Singapore) under

the supervision of MRM Graphics, Winslow, Buckinghamshire, UK

ACKNOWLEDGEMENT

I would like to thank my partner, Andrew, for all his hard work and support in
the design and preparation of the screens shown throughout this book.

CONTENTS

INTRODUCTION

Screens are both decorative and versatile. Traditionally, they were used to hide untidy or ugly areas, or provide privacy in certain areas of a room; these are still popular uses for screens, but the way we live today, and the need for more flexible living spaces, has provided a further use: as temporary room dividers. Screens are especially useful in a large open space – say in a loft conversion, a kitchen and dining room that have been knocked into one, or a bedsitting room. In fact, in any area where you want to maintain contact between the two aspects of a room, but would sometimes prefer to have the option of a more intimate setting in each one, rather than a big space.

My aim is to demonstrate how a great variety of different looks, textures and styles can be incorporated into a basic three-panel screen, simply by the use of varying decorative techniques. Whether you want a contemporary or a traditional look, you will find ideas for each and every room, and all the designs may be adapted or embellished according to taste or ability. The result, a unique and attractive screen that is all your own work.

Many decorating techniques are covered, including appliqué, decoupage, marbling and mosaic, and each technique is explained in detail. So, whether you are a complete amateur or an advanced craftsperson, there will be something here for you. If you do not wish to employ these techniques in screen making, you could use them to decorate any flat surface throughout your home, be it a table or chair or even a wall surface.

The screens have been arranged in order of complexity, so the three frame screens in the first chapter are the lightest and simplest to make. If you prefer to try something more challenging, there will be a solid MDF (medium density fibreboard) panel screen to suit you in the second chapter; bear in mind, though, that the MDF panels are heavy, and you will need help assembling the screen.

The solid panel screens included here are shaped, and some have decorative cut-outs. If you are a complete novice, with little equipment, you may prefer to follow the instructions for decorating a particular screen, but use unshaped MDF panels without the cut-outs, and get the panels cut to size by your supplier. Alternatively, you could skip the woodworking stage entirely, and buy a ready made screen blank from a specialist outlet. This need not detract from the success of your screen – in fact, I hope you will use these projects as a starting point, and adapt them in any way you please to produce the particular screen you want.

Materials and Equipment

At the beginning of each project I list the materials and equipment you will need to complete the screen. All are standard items and readily available, usually from DIY shops or specialist art shops nationwide.

The softwood for the frame screens, and the MDF for the solid panel screens, can be bought from DIY stores or timber merchants. As I mentioned before, MDF is weighty but it can be bought in standard-size 12mm (^{1}/2in) thick panels, 1.8m x 0.6m (6 x 2ft) like those I used. If you cannot find this size, you might prefer to buy the panels from a timber merchant; not only is this likely to be cheaper, but a timber merchant would probably cut the panels to size for you.

A workshop would be a definite advantage when making the panel screens but, if you don't have one, perhaps you could borrow a friend's, or even ask the friend to prepare the panels for you. If that isn't an option, be resourceful, and set up a makeshift arrangement in your garage or a spare room. As some of the panel screens take a week or more to make, anywhere that is well ventilated, has room for an old table or workbench, and has storage space would be suitable. Alternatively, you could work outside.

You will not need much equipment, and you probably have many of the tools, such as a saw, screwdriver or pliers, around the house already; if you don't have items like the jigsaw or drill, they are not expensive to buy. But, if you would rather not make the outlay, hire one, or again borrow from a friend.

In each project I list quantities of materials. These are meant as a guideline only, and are the amounts I needed to complete my standard-size screens. If you decide to vary the size or decoration of your screen, remember to adjust the materials accordingly.

Where I mention a paint colour, it is from the Dulux Vinyl Satin Finish paint range. But the colours specified are a guideline only, and you may want to use combinations that match an existing scheme.

Generally, use your common sense. When doing messy jobs, such as painting or gluing or spraying, be sure to protect surrounding areas. Newspaper is invaluable for this, and several layers are best. You can then fold up and dispose of the top wet or sticky sheets, and leave the fresh sheets underneath while the screen dries.

Safety

Throughout the book there are many different techniques described for making and decorating each screen. For the most part, these are simple and straightforward, requiring only ordinary DIY or art materials. There are, however, a number of safety techniques that should always be observed, and it is common sense to read the manufacturer's instructions carefully before using a product.

Masks

When working with MDF, whether cutting, sanding or filing, a protective dust mask must always be worn. This is because constant or heavy inhalation of the dust may be harmful. Cheap masks, specifically for MDF, are readily available from tool or DIY shops. Be sure to choose a mask that suits the purpose, i.e. one that prevents the inhalation of minute dust particles.

You should also wear a mask, and work in a well-ventilated area, when spraying metallic paint, as it is dangerous to inhale the vapour.

Glue guns

Glue guns are thermostatic and work by heating a stick of solid glue and letting the resultant viscous glue out at a controlled rate. You must treat them with respect as the glue is very hot and can cause a nasty blister if dropped on the skin. The glue has the advantage of not setting for a couple of seconds, so you have time for adjustment, and the resultant bond is good.

Protective gloves

Thick rubber gloves should be worn when using solvents such as turpentine, to protect your hands from staining and irritation.

Protective gloves should also be worn when handling rough or sharp materials, e.g. when cutting chicken wire for the 'French Rustic Screen' or ceramic tiles for the mosaics used on the 'Moroccan Screen' and 'Roman-style Screen'.

Protective goggles

Protective goggles should be worn as well, when cutting or breaking ceramic tiles. They are essential for shielding your eyes from flying shards, which could be extremely dangerous if one became lodged in your eye.

Power tools

While working with power tools such as drills and jigsaws, always read and observe the safety precautions given on the instructions for the tool. As an added precaution, the mains plug should be attached to a circuit breaker; then, if you should cut through the mains cable, you will be protected from electrocution.

Most of the other techniques described carry no safety warnings other than common sense, and any other thoughts or tips on safety are given, where they occur, in each chapter.

Measurements

Measurements are in metric, with imperial equivalents in brackets. Instances may be found where a metric measurement has fractionally varying imperial equivalents, usually within $1/16$in either way. This is because in each particular case the closest imperial equivalent has been given.

NEVER use a mixture of metric and imperial measurements – always use one or the other.

FRAME SCREENS

Woven
Ribbon

French
Rustic

Appliqué

HOW TO MAKE A FRAME SCREEN

The three frame screens shown in this chapter are much lighter than the solid panel screens which follow and, although by the very nature of their construction they are not as versatile as the panel screens, the projects I include show just how attractive a frame screen can be. Frame screens have the added advantage that they are quite simple and quick to make, with only the minimum of tools and equipment.

The measurements given here are for a three-frame screen, 163cm (5ft 4in) high, with each frame 52cm (20^1/2in) wide. I have assumed this is the size you will use for the three frame screen projects but you can of course vary the size of your screen, and adjust the materials accordingly.

MATERIALS AND EQUIPMENT

6 X 248CM (8FT) LENGTHS OF PREPARED,
UNTREATED SOFTWOOD,
32 X 19MM (1¹/₄ X ³/₄IN) APPROX.

SOFT PENCIL

RULER OR TAPE MEASURE

SAW

MEDIUM GRADE SANDPAPER

DRILL AND COUNTERSINK DRILL BIT

12 BRASS WOOD SCREWS
4.8 X 64MM (NO. 10 X 2¹/₂IN)

SCREWDRIVER

BRADAWL

WOOD GLUE

WORKBENCH OR SUITABLE FLAT SURFACE
ON WHICH TO CLAMP LENGTHS DURING
CONSTRUCTION

CLAMP

6 X 40MM (1¹/₂IN) BRASS BUTT HINGES
24 X ROUND HEAD, SLOTTED BRASS
SCREWS FOR HINGES, 3.5 X 12MM
(NO 6 X ¹/₂IN)

METHOD

Preparing the wood

1 First cut your lengths of softwood to size. From each length you can cut one side piece and one crosspiece, i.e. one length has sufficient wood for half a frame.

Place the wood on a flat surface, measure a 163cm (5ft 4in) length, and mark this measurement with a pencil. Clamp the length of wood onto your workbench, so that the end to be cut juts out over the end of the bench, and carefully saw along the pencil line.

Measuring the wood for the frames

It's best to use a soft pencil to mark up the wood, so you don't have to press too hard. It will then be easy to wipe off the marks later, and you won't risk indenting the surface of the wood.

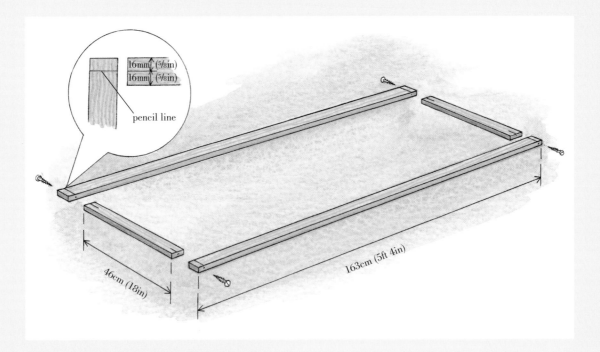

16mm (⅝in)
16mm (⅝in)

pencil line

46cm (18in)

163cm (5ft 4in)

2 Take the shorter piece that you have just cut and mark 46cm (18in) along its length. Cut off this length as before, discarding any excess. You now have two pieces that make up one half of the first screen panel.

Repeat with another length of the softwood, so that you have two long side pieces and two shorter crosspieces. Sand the rough areas of the cut ends until smooth.

Sanding the rough edges

Marking the position for the screws

3 Before these pieces can be joined, you must mark the position for the wood screw. Find a completely level surface, and lay one of the side pieces – widest edge down – at right angles to one of the crosspieces – also widest edge down; make sure that the top edges are aligned. With a pencil, mark a horizontal line on the top, wider, edge of the long piece, to directly correspond with the centre of the end of the crosspiece abutting it. Remove the long length, turn it on its side and re-mark the pencil line on the narrower edge that is now uppermost. Find the mid-point of this edge and, using a ruler, draw a line down which will intersect the previous line. Where these two lines cross should be the exact mid-point through which to drill the screw hole *(see diagram above)*.

4 Clamp the long length onto the bench, with the marked point for the screw uppermost. Select a suitable drill bit to accommodate the diameter of the screw, so that the screw will drop through the hole easily, and drill a hole right through the edge of the wood.

5 Next, countersink the drilled hole, to prevent the screw protruding from the side of the finished frame. Attach a countersink drill bit to your drill and place it over the original hole; drill carefully until you have a suitable indentation, which the head of the screw will sit in neatly.

Countersinking screw holes

Marking the pilot hole on the crosspiece

6 Before the two pieces of wood can be joined, you need to make a corresponding pilot hole in the end of the crosspiece. Place the two pieces at right angles to each other on a level surface, top edges aligned as before, and push the screw into the previously drilled hole. Holding the two pieces firmly together, gently tap the edge of the screw with a hammer to make an indentation into the end of the crosspiece. This will mark the position of the pilot hole.

7 Separate the pieces, and this time place the crosspiece vertically in a clamp, so that the pilot hole can be drilled into the end from above. Using a smaller drill bit than before, drill carefully into the end of the wood for approximately 25mm (1in). Remove the crosspiece from the clamp, ready for assembly.

8 Next, smear a small amount of wood glue onto the cut and drilled end of the crosspiece. This will stop the pieces from twisting away from each other when they are screwed together, and will also ensure a firm joint.

Joining the side piece and the crosspiece

9 Push the screw through the countersunk hole on the outer edge of the long side piece, until it engages in the pilot hole in the end of the crosspiece. Holding the two firmly together, screw into the pilot hole carefully, using a suitable screwdriver, until the two pieces are butted firmly up to each other. Make sure that they are properly aligned, and not twisted, before leaving the glue to set for at least an hour.

Repeat the process on all the other lengths of wood, until you have the three frames for your screen.

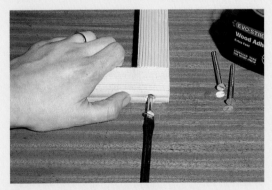

Screwing together the frame pieces

Although the frames will be separated for decoration, the hinges must be attached to the central panel, and screw holes for the hinges drilled in the side panels, before decorating. This will ensure that the hinges can be reattached with minimum disturbance to the panels once the frames have been decorated.

Positioning the hinges

10 First, mark out the exact position for the hinges to be fixed on both side edges of the central frame. Three x 40mm (1^1/$_2$in) brass butt hinges will be needed on each side. To find the position for the top hinge, measure 5cm (2in) down from the top of the frame, and to find the position for the bottom hinge, measure 10cm (4in) from the bottom edge of the frame. The middle hinge should be equidistant between the other two.

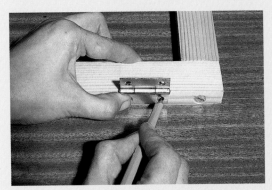

Marking out hinge placement

11 When attaching the hinges to the central frame, place each in turn and mark the screw holes using a pencil, making sure that each hinge is perfectly straight. Remove the hinge and mark a slight indentation over the pencil mark with a bradawl. This will stop the drill bit running off course during drilling, and ensure the hole is in its precise location.

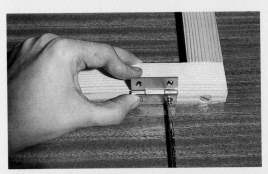

Attaching the hinges

12 Drill the holes for the hinges using an appropriate drill bit; take care to keep the drill straight at all times, so that the screw does not go into the resulting hole at an angle. Reposition the hinges as you go, and use a screwdriver to tighten the screws and fix the hinges in place. Continue down both sides of the central panel, until all the hinges have been attached.

Note: the hinges placed down one side of the panel must open in the opposite way to the hinges down the other side so that, once all panels are fastened together, the screen can fold flat, and will open in a concertina fashion.

Attaching the hinges

13 To complete the screen, the frames must be stood upright, on a completely level surface. Make sure that the bottom edges of the panels are aligned properly, so that the screen will stand up safely when the frames are joined together.

First, stand the central frame upright, then bring one of the side frames alongside at an angle of about 45°. Hold the frames together at the top, taking care that they are both vertical and close to each other all the way down; mark the screw holes for the top hinge on the side frame with pencil and bradawl. Remove the side frame and drill the holes as before. Bring back the side frame and attach the top hinge to it. This will allow the two frames to stand freely on their own, and enable you to mark and drill the other hinges along that same edge.

When you have attached one side frame, repeat the process on the other side until all three are fastened together.

14 You are now ready to complete the frames with the finish of your choice but, before doing so, unscrew the hinges to separate them. The frames will be easier to decorate singly and they can be reattached quickly once decoration is complete.

Applying a finish to the wood

If you fancy an unadorned, natural look, the wood can be left untreated. But, if you favour something more mellow, finish the wood with soft liquid wax (see 'Appliquéd Fabric Screen', on page 23), or with two coats of matt acrylic varnish.

For a bolder, more colourful effect, paint the wood with satin emulsion in a colour to complement, or contrast with, your chosen decoration (see 'French Rustic Screen', on page 17).

But, if you're feeling more adventurous, try a colour-washed effect, which will change the colour of the wood, but still allow the grain to show through.

To achieve this look, apply a generous coat of diluted emulsion to the wood; wait 15 minutes or so, then wipe away the excess paint with a soft cloth to reveal the grain. Once the paint is dry, seal the paintwork with a protective coat of matt acrylic varnish.

WOVEN RIBBON
FRAME SCREEN

Can be completed in a day

This attractive screen is simple to make and, by varying the type and colour of ribbon used, it can be adapted to make a charming and effective addition to any room in the home.

For a lounge or bedroom, it would be better to choose the classic look and rich colour of the satin ribbon used here, but for a kitchen or bathroom, the whole look and feel of the screen could be altered dramatically by using fresher colours and textures. Bear in mind that combining different widths of ribbon will create more variety, while closely woven ribbons provide more privacy. My screen used about 40m (130ft) of each ribbon but, obviously, the closer the ribbons are together, the more you will use, so it is impossible to say exactly how much of each colour you will need for your screen.

Whatever you choose, you will find this screen takes little time and effort to make and is relatively inexpensive.

MATERIALS AND EQUIPMENT

FRAME SCREEN (SEE PAGE 6)

AT LEAST FOUR DIFFERENT COLOURS OF RIBBON – APPROXIMATELY ONE COMPLETE ROLL OF EACH

STAPLES AND STAPLE GUN

RULER

APPROX. 13M (14YD 6IN) BRAID TO MATCH RIBBONS, 12–18MM (¹/₂–³/₄IN) WIDE

RUBBER SOLUTION GLUE OR HOT MELT GLUE GUN

OPTIONAL: PALE SHADE OF LIQUID WAX FOR THE FRAME (E.G. 'PINE')

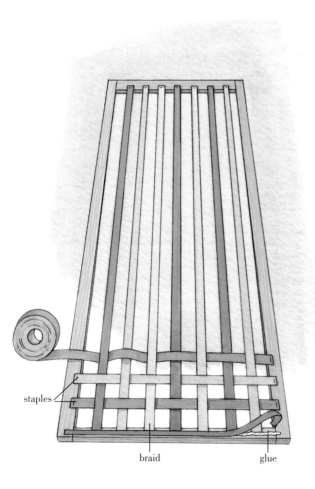

staples

braid   glue

METHOD

1 Wax the frame if you wish (see 'Applying a finish to the wood', on page 11). I have left mine untreated, to give a more contemporary look.

Attaching the longer lengths of ribbon

Lay the frames down on a hard flat surface, to prevent them bouncing as you staple on the ribbon.
Don't worry if the ribbons are too loose, or you make a mistake – the staples can be removed easily, by first lifting them with a small screwdriver, then pulling them out with pliers.

2 Choose your first colour of ribbon, but do not cut it yet. Attach the loose end of ribbon to the top of the frame with one staple, then, holding onto the rest of the roll, pull the ribbon tight while you staple it to the bottom of the frame. Cut off the strip and continue in this way, changing the colours when required, until the width of the frame is filled with the vertical ribbons.

If you prefer, you could use offcuts of ribbon. This would create a pleasingly random effect, as well as cutting the cost.

If the spacing between the ribbons is important, you will get a neater effect by measuring the spaces with a ruler.

Sticking down the braid

3 Next, add the crosspieces. Take the loose end of the first roll of ribbon and weave it through the other longer lengths, moving in and out of each strip alternately, until the opposite side of the frame is reached. Secure the cut end of ribbon with a staple, then pull the roll across the width, to keep the ribbon tight in the frame. Anchor the length at the other side with a staple, then cut off the excess. Repeat this process across the rest of the frame, weaving each strip through alternately and repeating the colours to form a sequence. When you have completed one frame, continue the process with the other frames until all are covered.

4 Once the ribbons are attached to the frames, cover up the stapled edges with the braid. Cut separate strips of braid for the sides, top and bottom of each frame, remembering to allow a turn in at each end. Apply some glue to the top of the first frame side to be covered, turn under the end of the braid, and press it down into the glue, taking care to keep the braid parallel with the sides of the frame. Make sure the braid is fixed firmly in place, then continue to apply glue to the frame and ease the braid down along the full length. Remember to finish all cut ends by turning them under, and gluing them down to prevent fraying.

Weaving the ribbon across the frame

5 Once the braid has been fixed, reattach the hinges to the frame (see instructions on page 10), and your screen is ready for use.

FRENCH RUSTIC SCREEN

with gingham curtain and chicken wire

Allow 2 days to complete

This delightful screen, simple in style and decoration, will add colour and texture to any room where the emphasis is on plain old-fashioned country charm. But the use of gingham curtains and chicken wire, inspired by the rustic French country look, make it especially suitable for a kitchen or bathroom.

MATERIALS AND EQUIPMENT

FRAME SCREEN (SEE PAGE 6)

BLUE SATIN EMULSION PAINT TO MATCH GINGHAM FABRIC

SOFT LIQUID WAX IN A MEDIUM BROWN SHADE, E.G. 'LIGHT OAK'

FINE GRADE WIRE WOOL

RUBBER GLOVES AND HEAVY-DUTY PROTECTIVE GLOVES
(not shown in photographs)

CHICKEN WIRE, APPROX. 5M (16FT 6IN)

MARKER PEN

WIRE CUTTERS FOR THE CHICKEN WIRE

SMALL STAPLE NAILS AND HAMMER OR HEAVY DUTY STAPLES AND STAPLE GUN

BLUE GINGHAM FABRIC, APPROX. 5M (16FT 3IN), 90CM (35$\frac{1}{2}$IN) WIDE

MATCHING THREAD FOR SEWING

EXPANDABLE CURTAIN WIRE, APPROX. 3M (3YD 9IN)

HOOKS AND EYELETS FOR THE CURTAIN WIRE: 12 HOOKS AND 12 EYELETS

OPTIONAL: 18 ADDITIONAL HOOKS, (IN CASE THE CURTAIN SAGS)

PLIERS

BLUE BRAID TO MATCH PAINT AND FABRIC (OPTIONAL), APPROX. 13M (14YD 6IN) LONG X 12–18MM ($\frac{1}{2}$–$\frac{3}{4}$IN) WIDE

RUBBER SOLUTION GLUE OR HOT MELT GLUE GUN

If possible, use staple nails to attach the chicken wire to the frame. They are hammered in, and enable you to pull the wire tightly across the frame, and anchor it in position.

METHOD

1 Paint all sides and edges of each frame with the blue emulsion paint and leave to dry for at least two hours.

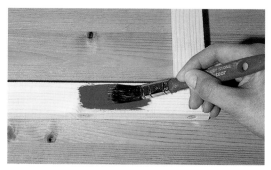

Painting the frame

2 Soften the liquid wax a little, by placing its container in warm water for a few minutes. Shake the container periodically, so the wax mixes well and flows easily from the container.

3 Then, wearing rubber gloves, apply a small amount of wax to a pad of wire wool. Rub the wax gently into the painted surface of each frame, working along the grain of the wood to achieve a smooth surface. The wire wool should remove all rough areas from the wood, leaving it smooth to the touch, and the colour of the wax will slightly darken the paint to achieve a more rustic feel. Some of the paint may be removed during this process, but don't worry, as this will add to the overall look. Wax the other panels in the same way, then leave them all to dry.

Applying the wax

If you want a little extra sheen, buff up the frames with a soft cloth once the wax has dried.

4 Next, prepare the chicken wire. Wearing heavy-duty gloves to protect your hands from the sharp edges, roll out sufficient wire to overlap the window area of the frame on all sides by an extra 2cm (approx. 3/4in). Use a marker pen to mark the final width on the wire, and the total length on the uncut end.

Do not cut the chicken wire longer than necessary, as re-cutting it later could be difficult.

5 Snip through the measured length and width of the roll with the wire cutters, using the pattern of the wire as a guide. Cut as neatly as possible, aiming to leave no sharp edges or points. Mark off wire for the other two frames in the same way. N.B. It is extremely important to maintain straight lines, so that the wire runs straight down the length of the frame on both sides. If, after attachment, you find the wire is not straight, you will have to remove the staples with a screwdriver and a pair of pliers, which could ultimately make a mess of the frame and ruin the finish.

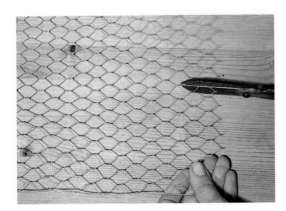

Cutting the chicken wire

Attaching the chicken wire is quite a time-consuming job, but it is important to fix it on well. Lay the frame flat on a hard surface to prevent it from springing up during stapling.

6 Still wearing your protective gloves, start fixing the chicken wire to the top corner of each frame. Work along the width of the frame, spacing the staples at approximately 2.5cm (1in) intervals. It is essential that the wire is laid correctly on the frame, so check as you go that it is still in alignment, and will cover the long sides of the frame as well as the bottom edge.

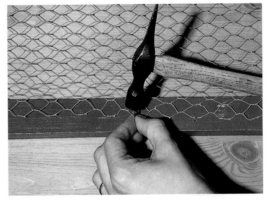

Attaching the chicken wire to the frame

7 Once the wire has been attached to the top, secure it down the sides, then along the bottom.

If, after fastening the wire to the frame, there are still some sharp edges, you can cover these and hide the staples with matching braid.

8 Measure lengths of braid for the four sides, allowing for a turn-in at each end. Turn under the end of the first length of braid then, using a rubber solution glue or hot melt glue gun, glue along the edges of the frame, gradually pressing the braid onto the glue as you go. Finish the other end in the same way, turning the braid under neatly before gluing it down. Repeat on all the wire edges of each panel.

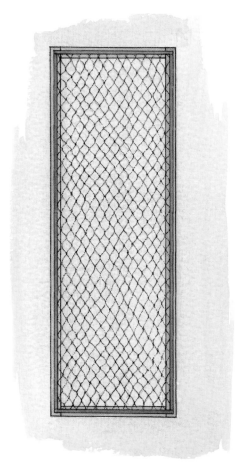

9 Next, make the curtains. To find the correct length of fabric, measure the finished height of your frame and add on 3cm (1¼in) to the measurement. Mark the same measurement on the fabric and cut out three matching pieces, one for each frame.

NOTE: the width of the fabric must be at least 1¹/2 times the width of the screen, to allow for gathering.

10 With the curtain fabric wrong side up, turn in 1cm (³/8in) down each side, and then the same amount again, to create double seams. Pin and tack the double seams in position, then machine-sew with a medium stitch. Remove the tacking thread and press each seam with a hot iron. Repeat on the other two pieces of fabric.

11 Again place one curtain wrong-side-up, and make pockets top and bottom, to take the curtain wire. Turn in 1.5cm (⁵/8in) at each end of the fabric, and then repeat to create a double hem. Pin the pockets in position and check that they are wide enough to take the curtain hook. If they are not wide enough, adjust the width of the pockets, making sure that the fabric is still long enough to cover the whole of the frame. Tack the pockets along the pinned line, then stitch along the inner edges of the hems, again with a medium machine stitch. Repeat on the other curtains and press the pockets with a hot iron.

12 Next, lay the frames face down (stapled sides up) and, with a bradawl or sharp tool, mark holes for the curtain eyelets, approximately 1.5cm (⁵/8in) in from the edges of the frames, in each of the four corners. Screw an eyelet in each hole, making sure each one ends up sitting vertically.

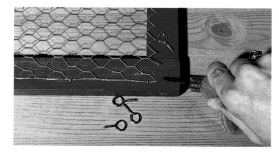

Making holes for the eyelets

If you hold the curtain wire firmly with pliers, it's easier to screw the hook into the end.

13 To measure the curtain wire, first screw a hook into the loose end of the wire, then attach this hook to one of the eyelets fixed on the frame. Stretch the wire tightly across the width of the frame until it reaches the screw eyelet on the other side. Mark this length on the wire.

Fastening hooks into the curtain wire

The final length of wire should be approximately 1cm ($^3/_8$ in) shorter than the piece you have measured. This is to stop the wire sagging with the weight of the fabric, when it is stretched tightly across the frame.

---

14 Cut the wire with wire cutters or pliers, and attach another screw hook into the cut end. Repeat the process with the other five lengths of wire.

Cutting the curtain wire

15 Thread a length of wire through the pockets in each curtain, and gather the fabric evenly along the width.

Threading the curtain wire

16 To attach the curtains to the frames, place the curtains hemmed side down and hook the lengths of wire to the eyelets already in position.

If you find the wire sags and the curtains dip in the middle, you can screw in additional hooks, in line with those at each side, and latch the pocketed curtain wire over these.

---

17 Attach the hinges (see instructions on page 10), and your screen is complete.

Appliqued Fabric Screen

Allow 2 days to complete

This is a very pretty screen, with a luxurious look and feel that would suit a feminine bedroom or bathroom. The metallic gold stitches around the appliquéd pieces add a glamorous finishing touch, while the diaphanous backing curtain gives it an ethereal quality.

The look of this screen relies heavily on more traditional designs for its inspiration, and 'cottage garden' flowered panels, as shown here, are especially suitable for the appliqué. For the backing curtains I have used plain striped, sheer nylon curtain fabric but, whatever you choose, bear in mind that the fabric should be quite robust, as well as sheer.

The appliqué will be easier to cut out, and more effective, if you choose a fabric with a large and bold design.

MATERIALS AND EQUIPMENT

FRAME SCREEN (SEE PAGE 6)

SOFT LIQUID WAX

RUBBER GLOVES

FINE GRADE WIRE WOOL

SCISSORS WITH SHARP POINTS

SHEER WHITE BACKING FABRIC
(E.G. NYLON) APPROX. 7M (7³/₄YD) LONG,
137CM (54IN) WIDE

FABRIC REMNANTS IN BOLD FLOWERY
DESIGNS TO FORM APPLIQUÉD PANELS

BOND-A-WEB TO ATTACH APPLIQUE PANELS
TO BACKING FABRIC

IRON

NON-STICK BAKING PAPER
(not shown in photographs)

METALLIC GOLD THREAD FOR
MACHINE SEWING

FINE WHITE THREAD (SUITABLE FOR
CHOSEN BACKING FABRIC)

EXPANDABLE CURTAIN WIRE,
APPROX. 3.5M (11FT 6IN)

12 HOOKS AND EYELETS TO ATTACH
CURTAIN WIRE TO FRAME

---

*First, finish the plain wooden frame
with the soft liquid wax.
To soften the wax, and make it run more
freely, place the container in warm water
for a few minutes, and shake it
periodically to mix well.*

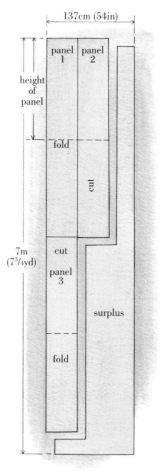

The diagram shows how you can achieve three double thickness curtains from your length of fabric.

METHOD

1 Put on rubber gloves for protection, and squeeze a little wax onto a small pad of wire wool. Work the wax into the surface of the frame, always working along the grain of the wood until it has a silky smooth finish. Leave the wax to dry for at least one hour, then buff up the surface with a soft cloth, to give it an extra sheen. Finish the other two frames in the same way.

2 Next, cut the sheer white fabric for the backing curtains, bearing in mind each frame has a double thickness curtain. To calculate the length of backing fabric for each curtain, measure the finished height of one frame, add on 5cm (2in) for hems, and double the final figure. To calculate the curtain width, measure the width of a frame and add on 2.5cm (1in) for side seams.

3 Decide whether your three panels will be identical in design, or whether the centre one will dominate over the two side panels, as my design does. Then select the images you want to appliqué on each panel, and cut roughly around the shapes; you will cut more carefully around the intricate areas in stage 6.

Cutting out fabric pieces for the appliqué

4 Pin your cut appliqué pieces onto Bond-a-web. Bond-a-web enables you to bond one layer of fabric to another, and makes it easier to stitch around the edges of the appliqué later. Make sure the shiny side of the Bond-a-web is in contact with the wrong side of the appliqué fabric, then cut the Bond-a-web around the pinned images. Make sure there are no exposed areas of Bond-a-web, as these would melt onto the iron.

Use a piece of non-stick baking paper on the ironing surface, and between the iron and the piece being bonded, to protect the work surface and iron. If the fabric piece does get stuck to the ironing board, gently peel it away before it cools.

---

5 With the fabric side uppermost, press the fabric pieces firmly with a moderately hot iron, so the surface of the Bond-a-web melts, and the appliqué pieces are bonded to it. Remember to remove the pins gradually, as you go.

Ironing appliqué pieces onto Bond-a-web

6 When the pieces are firmly attached, carefully cut around the intricate areas of the appliqué pieces, and peel off the Bond-a-web backing sheet, so that the adhesive is exposed.

Cutting around the appliqué images

7 Fold one piece of backing fabric in half lengthways (i.e. with a fold at the top, and two raw edges at the bottom), right side out. Iron to mark where the fold occurs, then open out the fabric. Repeat with the other two fabric panels.

8 Next, position your images to be appliquéd – on the front half of the curtain only, as the back will not be appliquéd – remembering that the Bond-a-webbed side of the fabric pieces must be in contact with the right side of the backing curtain. Repeat the positioning process with the other two pieces of backing fabric, making sure that the images will align on all three panels where required, and that the design will be balanced when the screen is finished.

NOTE: it is essential that the backing fabric is single, not doubled over, when you iron on the appliqué pieces. This is especially so when using a sheer backing fabric, as the adhesive from the Bond-a-web will easily soak through all layers of fabric, and you risk unsightly glue marks on the fabric used on the back panel.

9 When you are happy with the layout, pin and tack each image in position. Then, using non-stick paper to protect the surfaces as before, use a moderately hot iron on the surface of the images to attach them to the backing fabric.

Ironing the images onto the backing curtain

10 Once all the pieces are securely attached, add a finishing touch by machine-sewing a zigzag stitch around the edges of each piece, using the metallic gold thread. Again, be sure that the curtain is in a single layer, and that you only machine through the front half.

Zigzagging around the appliqué with metallic thread

When machining the images onto the backing, take care to follow exactly the contours of each appliquéd piece. Use a fairly close stitch, but make sure that the tension is not too tight, or the backing fabric will pucker.

11 Next, make up the backing curtains. Locate the centre fold you ironed in each curtain (the fold will form the top of the curtain) and refold, so the curtain is right side out, with the appliqué on the outside. Then form the top pocket for the curtain wire, by pinning a line, 2.5cm (1in) down from the folded edge. Check the pocket is wide enough to take the curtain hook, tack, then machine-stitch along this line.

12 To hide any untidy areas of stitching, the backing curtains are machine-stitched to form bags. To do this, turn the curtain over, so the pocket and appliqué are now on the inside and the wrong sides are facing out. Starting below the line of stitching which forms the pocket (so you don't machine the ends of the curtain wire pocket), pin and tack 1.5cm (⁵/₈in) wide seams down each long edge, then machine along the tacked lines with the white thread.

13 Turn the bag right side out, so the appliqué is now on the outside and – ensuring again that you don't stitch over the ends of the pocket – top-stitch down each long edge, 0.5cm (²/8in) in from the side, to give a neat finish. From now on the bag remains right side out.

14 To form the pocket for the lower curtain wire, turn the bottom, open ends of the curtains over twice, to form a 1.5cm (⁵/8in) double hem on the back of each curtain. Pin and tack along the inner fold line to form the pocket, checking that it's wide enough to take the curtain hook, before machine-stitching.

15 Press all seams with a warm iron. Take care that you don't iron over the appliqué, as this could melt the Bond-a-web and spoil the finished result. Finish off any raw areas with hand-stitching, to prevent fraying.

16 The curtains are attached to the frame using expandable curtain wire. First, with a bradawl or sharp tool, mark holes for the eyelets, approximately 1.5cm (⁵/8in) in from the four corners of each frame. Screw an eyelet in each hole, making sure each one ends up sitting vertically.

Holding the curtain wire firmly with pliers makes it easier to screw the hook into the end, but make sure the outer coating of the wire is not removed while twisting in the hook.

---

17 To measure the curtain wire, first screw a hook into the loose end of the wire, then attach the hook to one of the eyelets in the frame and stretch it tightly across the width of the frame, until it reaches the eyelet on the other side. Mark this length on the wire.

NOTE: the final length of wire should be approximately 1cm (³/8in) shorter than the piece you have measured. This is to stop the wire sagging with the weight of the fabric, when it is stretched tightly across the frame.

18 Cut the wire with wire cutters or pliers and attach another screw hook into the cut end. Repeat the process for all the lengths of wire.

19 Thread each length of wire through the pockets in the fabric and attach the curtains to the frames by hooking the lengths of wire to the eyelets already in position.

Threading through the curtain wire

20 You can now attach the hinges to the frames (see page 10), and your screen is complete.

Attaching the curtain to the frame

SOLID PANEL SCREENS

Country-look

Decoupage

Leather-effect

Wallpapered

Upholstered

Verdigris

Driftwood

Moroccan

Music Score

Roman-style

HOW TO MAKE A SOLID PANEL SCREEN

Solid panel screens are much more robust and versatile than the frame screens featured in the previous chapter, as the shape of the panel can be transformed with elaborate curves and scrolls, ornamental shapes can be cut in the panel itself, and the surface can be treated with all manner of decoration. However, panel screens are also much heavier and more bulky than frame screens, and therefore constitute a more challenging and serious piece of furniture, requiring additional skills, and assistance when assembling the screen.

The solid panel screen projects that follow assume you will make the standard three-panel screen described here, which is approximately 1.8m (6ft) high, and has three panels, each 0.6m (2ft) wide.

The designs for the different screens are provided on gridded templates (see pages 107–117). In order to transfer a design from a template to a panel, the design must be scaled up, using a gridded paper pattern that exactly fits the screen panel. Instructions for making the paper pattern are given on the facing page.

Before attempting a solid panel screen, bear in mind that MDF dust is dangerous and great care must be taken. A mask must be worn at all times when cutting or sanding MDF, and the work should be carried out in a workshop, or a well-ventilated area, ideally the garden. Never try to sweep up the dust – always use a vacuum cleaner. If you do not have a workshop yourself, perhaps you can persuade a friend to let you use theirs, or even prepare the panels for you!

MATERIALS AND EQUIPMENT

3 PIECES OF 12MM ($^1/_2$IN) MDF, EACH APPROX. 1.8M X 0.6M (6FT X 2FT)

WORKBENCH OR TABLE AND SUITABLE MEANS OF CLAMPING PANELS TO SURFACE

ROLL OF GREASEPROOF PAPER FOR THE PAPER PATTERN

MASKING TAPE OR STICKY TAPE

PENCIL

BALLPOINT PEN

RULER

SCISSORS

CARBON PAPER

TAPE MEASURE

DRILL WITH BIT LARGE ENOUGH TO MAKE A HOLE TO TAKE THE JIGSAW BLADE – THIS IS NECESSARY WHEN CUTTING PANELS WITH CUT-OUT SHAPES

JIGSAW WITH SMALL (7CM / 2$^3/_4$IN) BLADE FOR CUTTING SCROLLS

DUST MASK

LARGE FILE, MEDIUM GRADE

MEDIUM AND FINE GRADE SANDPAPER

BRASS BUTT HINGES: 6 X 40MM (1$^1/_2$IN)

24 ROUND HEAD SLOTTED BRASS SCREWS FOR HINGES: 3.5 X 12MM (NO.6 X $^1/_2$IN)

N.B. THE 'MOROCCAN' AND 'ROMAN-STYLE' SCREENS WILL EACH NEED 6 HEAVIER, 50MM (2IN) HINGES AND 24 ROUND HEAD SLOTTED BRASS SCREWS 4 X 20MM (NO.8 X $^3/_4$IN)

DRILL

SCREWDRIVER

BRADAWL

METHOD

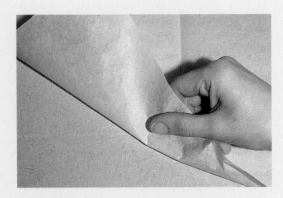

Making a paper pattern

1 First make a pattern, exactly the same size as a panel front, out of greaseproof paper. To do this, lay one of your MDF panels on a flat surface, and cover with a sheet of greaseproof paper. If the paper is not sufficiently wide to cover the panel from edge to edge, join two pieces lengthways, using masking or sticky tape. Then, line up one side of the paper along the top of the panel, and one along the left (long) edge of the panel, and secure the paper at intervals with small pieces of tape. If the paper is now larger than the panel, you must cut off the excess. To mark the amount to be cut off, pull the paper down over the unsecured edges of the panel, and run your fingers along the edges, creasing the paper as you go. Apply firm pressure to obtain as sharp a crease as possible, then cut along the crease lines with scissors. The paper should now be exactly the same size as the panel front.

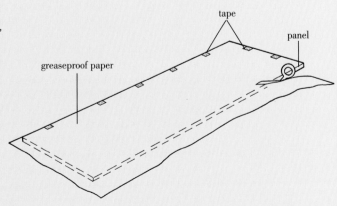

tape

panel

greaseproof paper

2 Next, mark the lines for the grid on the greaseproof. To do this, remove the small pieces of tape from the edges of the paper pattern, and fold the paper carefully to form the squares of the grid. First, fold the paper in half lengthways and then in half lengthways again. Press the creases in firmly and make sure that the paper is folded accurately, as the grid lines must be straight. You should now have three vertical creased lines down the entire length of the paper (A). Then, with the paper still folded, fold again, in half widthwise. Do two more folds in this direction, folding the paper in half each time (B). When you open the pattern flat again you are left with 32 squares across the whole of the sheet (C). These lines will form the lines of your grid.

3 Open out the paper pattern on a hard flat surface then, using a ballpoint pen or pencil and ruler, draw in the grid lines to make them more visible. Repeat over all the creases, until each is clearly outlined.

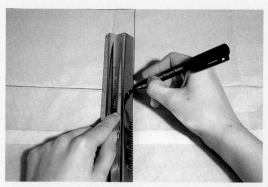

Marking out lines on the paper pattern for the grid

4 Next, transfer the chosen design from the gridded template to the paper pattern (see templates on pages 107–117). The easiest way to do this is to copy the template onto the paper pattern one square at a time, exactly reproducing the lines placed in each square. It is best to use a pencil for this, so that you can rub out any mistakes. Continue copying each square in this way, until you are left with a scaled up version of the original design on the paper pattern.

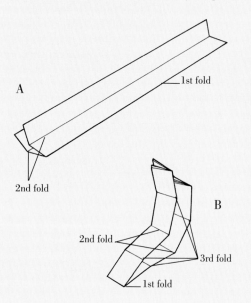

A

1st fold

2nd fold

2nd fold

B

3rd fold

1st fold

C

finished grid unfolded

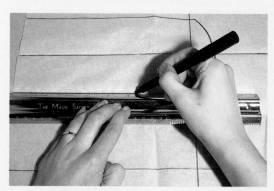

Drawing on design over the grid

5 To transfer the design from the paper pattern to the MDF, lay the pattern back on the panel, and secure it once more with small pieces of tape placed at intervals along the top and left edges. Then take a piece of carbon paper, and place it carbon side down between the paper pattern and the MDF, underneath the area that you wish to transfer. Trace over the lines on the paper pattern with a pencil, so that the carbon image is transferred to the panel. When you have traced over one area, move the carbon paper along slightly and trace over the next area of the panel, until the whole design has been transferred. Remove the paper pattern from the first panel and repeat the whole process on the other two panels. Remember to reverse the designs where necessary, for example for the 'Driftwood' and 'Music Score' screens, where the two outer panels need to be mirror images of each other.

CAUTION: A PROTECTIVE MASK MUST BE WORN AT ALL TIMES WHEN CUTTING, FILING OR SANDING MDF, TO AVOID INHALATION OF HARMFUL DUST.

Transferring design to panel using carbon paper

Transferring the verdigris pattern to the panel

Shaping the edges of the panels

6 Once the designs have been transferred to the panels, you can shape the panel edges with the jigsaw. First, clamp the panel to a workbench or suitable surface to keep it firmly in position while cutting. Make sure the area you wish to cut overhangs the edge of the bench or table, to avoid cutting through the table with the blade. Place the jigsaw blade on the line you wish to cut and, holding it firmly, gently depress the switch. Hold the jigsaw as steady as you can and do not try to cut too fast. Always keep the guide plate flat against the surface of the MDF during cutting, to keep good control of the jigsaw and, following the carbon line, cut carefully around the edges and curves. Don't worry if the lines are not quite perfect; small imperfections can be filed away later.

If you find it difficult to cut into a deep curve by sawing continuously round the carbon line, remove your finger from the jigsaw switch, take the jigsaw out of the cut, and approach the line from the opposite direction. You can then cut into the curve, instead of along it.

Cutting out shapes from the middle of a panel

7 If your chosen design requires shapes to be cut out from the middle of a panel, you will need to drill a pilot hole for the blade to slot into. Select a drill bit that will make a hole large enough for the blade to sit in comfortably, place the blade in the hole, and cut out as before. Repeat for the other two panels.

Drilling pilot holes for jigsawing cut-outs

8 The next stage is to tidy up any areas that have not been cut straight. Use a medium file for this, and gently file away the imperfections. Take great care to keep the file at right angles to the panel, so that you achieve a nice straight edge. Repeat on each panel until you are satisfied with the resulting shape.

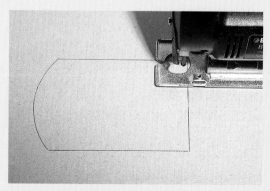

Jigsawing out the holes

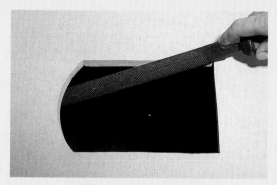

Filing rough edges

9 After cutting and filing each panel, you can remove any remaining rough areas with sandpaper. Begin with a medium grade paper, then finish with a fine grade, until you have achieved a smooth finish.

Sanding rough edges

NOTE: although the panels will be separated for decoration, the hinges must be attached to the central panel, and the screw holes for the hinges drilled in the side panels, before decorating. This will ensure that the hinges can be reattached with minimum disturbance to the panels once the panels have been decorated. This applies to all solid panel screens except the 'Wallpapered Screen' and 'Upholstered Screen'. Because these two have braid around the edges, the hinges must be positioned and fixed after the screens have been decorated.

Positioning the hinges

NOTE: remember that the 'Moroccan Screen' and 'Roman-style Screen', which are tiled, should have slightly larger, 50mm (2in) hinges, and larger screws to take the extra weight of the panels.

10 First, mark out the exact position for the hinges to be fixed on both side edges of the central panel. Three brass butt hinges will be needed on each side. To find the position for the top hinges, measure 5cm (2in) down from where the straight side begins, and to find the position for the bottom hinges, measure 10cm (4in) from the bottom edge of the panel. The middle hinge should be equidistant from the other two.

NOTE: the hinges placed down one side of the central panel must open in the opposite way to the hinges down the other side; this will ensure that, once the three panels are fastened together, the screen can fold flat, and will open out in a concertina fashion.

Attaching the hinges

11 When attaching the hinges to the central panel, place each in turn and mark the screw holes using a pencil, making sure that each hinge is perfectly straight. Remove the hinge and mark a slight indentation over the pencil mark with a bradawl. This will stop the drill bit running off course during drilling, and ensure the hole is in its precise location.

12 When drilling the holes for the hinges, use an appropriate drill bit and take care to keep the drill straight at all times; this will ensure that the screw, also, will go in straight. Reposition the hinges as you go, and use a screwdriver to tighten the screws as you fix the hinges in place. Continue down both sides of the central panel, until all hinges have been attached.

13 To complete the screen, the panels must be stood upright, on a completely level surface. This will ensure that the bottom edges of the panels align properly, and that the screen will stand up safely when the panels are joined together. Because of the weight of the panels you will probably need assistance at this stage, so make sure help is available before you start.

Stand the central panel up first, then bring one of the side panels alongside it at an angle of about 45°. Hold the panels together at the top, taking care that they are both vertical and close to each other all the way down, then mark the screw holes for the top hinge on the side panel, with the pencil and bradawl. Remove the side panel and drill the holes as before. Bring back the side panel and attach the top hinge to it. This will allow the two panels to stand freely on their own and you can then mark and drill the other hinges along that same edge.

When you have attached one side panel, attach the other side panel in the same way, so that all three are fastened together.

14 You are now ready to decorate the panels but, before doing so, unscrew the hinges to separate the panels. The panels will be easier to decorate singly, and they can be reattached easily once decoration has been completed.

COUNTRY-LOOK SCREEN

with cut-outs and stencils

Allow 3–4 days to complete

This is an evocative screen, with aged paint effect, cut-outs and stencilled trailing ivy leaves reminiscent of an old-fashioned garden door in a country garden. The natural, vibrant colours make it particularly suitable for a kitchen, conservatory or bedroom, but it would look at home in any room.

You can of course use any stencil you like, but trailing ivy is especially appropriate, and you can buy a pre-cut stencil of this in many DIY shops. Alternatively, if you're feeling adventurous, you could make your own stencil, perhaps copying the one I've used here.

If you do decide to make your own stencil, you'll need to make it out of oiled Manila stencil paper, acetate or thick tracing paper. Use 'Trace-down' (available from art shops) to transfer your design to the stencil, or place a sheet of carbon paper between the design and the Manila paper, and draw over the design with a sharp pencil or ballpoint pen. Once the design has been traced, carefully cut out the stencil using a sharp craft knife and a cutting mat.

MATERIALS AND EQUIPMENT

SHAPED PANELS
(SEE TEMPLATE ON PAGE 108)

1 LITRE LIGHT GREEN SATIN
EMULSION PAINT

1 LITRE DARK GREEN SATIN
EMULSION PAINT

RED SATIN EMULSION PAINT

PRE-CUT STENCIL, E.G. TRAILING IVY,
LARGE ENOUGH TO COVER THE CORNER
OF ONE PANEL

MASKING TAPE

STENCIL BRUSH, SIZE 4 OR 6

MEDIUM AND FINE GRADE SANDPAPER

SMALL ARTISTS' BRUSH

CLEAR SATIN POLYURETHANE VARNISH

N.B. IF MAKING YOUR OWN STENCIL,
YOU WILL ALSO NEED OILED MANILA
STENCIL PAPER (ACETATE OR THICK
TRACING PAPER COULD ALSO BE USED),
'TRACE-DOWN' (OR CARBON PAPER),
A SHARP CRAFT KNIFE AND A CUTTING MAT

METHOD

When choosing the two shades of green paint, make sure that you have a definite contrast between the colours so that, on the final sanding of the top layer, the shade of green underneath will stand out.

1 First undercoat both sides and edges of each panel with the light green emulsion paint. Leave them to dry for 3–4 hours, or as long as recommended by the manufacturer.

Undercoating the panels with emulsion

2 Once the undercoat is completely dry, you may find the paint has raised the texture of the MDF slightly, making it rather rough to the touch. If so, sand all the surfaces back a little by hand, paying particular attention to the edges. First sand gently with the medium grade sandpaper then, when the surface feels smooth to the touch, sand with the finer grade, until the surface has a silky smooth feel.

3 Now apply a second coat of emulsion, this time using the dark green paint; remember, as before, to include all sides and edges. Leave the panels to dry for 3–4 hours. This top coat of paint should not raise the grain, so you won't need to sand the panels again to make them smooth.

Applying a top coat of dark green emulsion

4 Once the paint is properly dry, you can 'distress' the panels, by sanding back areas of the top layer of paint to reveal the lighter paint below. Use the fine grade sandpaper, and gently rub over the paint, concentrating on areas that would have worn and weathered naturally, e.g. the edges and small patches around the cut-outs in the wood. Sand until the light green undercoat paint is visible, but do not rub too hard as you will run the risk of sanding back both layers of paint and revealing the bare MDF underneath.

Sanding back the dark green emulsion

Don't forget the stencilled patterns on the right-hand side of each panel are a mirror image of those on the left-hand side, so the stencil must be reversed for the opposite corners.

5 When you are satisfied with your first panel, treat the other two in the same way. The next stage is to stencil your chosen design on the front of each panel.

6 Position your stencil design on the front of a screen panel, and secure it in place using small pieces of masking tape around the edges.

Positioning the stencil

To achieve even coverage when stencilling, always keep the brush at right angles to the surface. Also, to achieve a nice crisp image, make sure you completely cover the stencilled area, by stippling over the edges of the stencil surrounding your design.

7 Now you can stencil on your design. First, place a small amount of light green paint in a tray or container, and dip in the stencil brush to coat it with paint. Dab off the excess paint on kitchen paper, so that the brush is left quite dry; this is to stop the paint seeping under the edges of your stencil and spoiling the crisp image. Stipple the colour over one half of every leaf and stem, dabbing the brush up and down quite quickly until the given area is covered. Re-load the brush when necessary, repeating the process described above.

Creating a shaded effect with mid-green emulsion

Stencilling with the light green emulsion

Don't remove the stencil until all the colours have been applied in one corner, as it would be difficult to reposition it later.

Make sure you wash your stencil brush thoroughly between colours, or you'll risk spoiling the effect by contaminating one colour with another.

9 Leave the berries until last, and use the red emulsion for these, repeating the technique described above. When you have completed one corner, carefully peel back the stencil card to reveal the design.

Stencilling in the red berries

8 To give a shaded effect, fill in the remaining halves of the leaves and stems with an intermediate green, made by mixing some light green emulsion with some dark green emulsion. Continue stencilling with this mid-green until the leaves and stems are completely filled in.

Always clean the stencil with water and kitchen paper (or a damp cloth) after each corner has been completed. This will prevent paint build-up on the edges and remove any wet paint that may smudge onto another area of the screen.

10 Repeat the stencil design in all four corners of each screen panel, remembering to reverse the stencil on the opposite side of each panel, to achieve a 'mirror-image' effect.

Allow to dry completely before continuing with the next stage.

11 To give the stencil a little more interest and detail, you may like to paint in the veins of the leaves freehand with the dark green emulsion used to topcoat the panels.

Using a small artists' brush, carefully paint the centre vein of each leaf, then add the lateral veins, so that they radiate from the centre vein towards the leaf edge. Next paint a narrow green line along one edge of the stems, and paint around the berries to give them a rounder shape. You can also add detail to the fruit by adding a small dot of green on the base of each berry.

Painting on the details

If you find that your stencilling is a little smudged in places, sharpen up any rough lines using the artists' brush and the background colour. When you have done this, leave the paint to dry again completely.

---

12 To continue with the 'distressed' theme of the screen, and to create a more aged look, you can sand back areas of the stencilling to make it look a little worn. To do this, use the fine grade sandpaper and rub small areas of the stencilling gently so that the paint is erased a little and is not quite so crisp. To achieve the look you want, only sand back small areas at a time – you cannot replace areas that have been lost by too much sanding.

Rubbing back the stencilling for an 'aged' look

13 When you are satisfied with your design, coat each panel all over with at least two coats of hard-wearing polyurethane satin varnish, to preserve your hard work. Allow the first coat to dry thoroughly, before applying the next coat.

Varnishing the panels

14 The panels are now complete and, once thoroughly dry, you can attach the hinges (see detailed instructions on page 35).

LEATHER-EFFECT SCREEN

Allow at least 1 week to complete

The sumptuous and dignified finish on this screen is inspired by the tooled leather on old books, and it would look especially good in a rather formal setting, perhaps a study or dining room. The effect should be rich and muted, not brash. Although I used brown for the screen shown here, a convincing leather effect could also be achieved with dark green or burgundy, for example.

Gold tooling is simulated by spraying gold paint through lace. It is important that the gold paint is acrylic, as other kinds might be dissolved by the white spirit when artists' oil colour is applied at a later stage. The lace should be large enough to cover an entire panel, so an old lace curtain would be ideal; a small, repetitive lace pattern is best, as this will produce the most convincing tooled effect. To make your screen even more authentic, you can add a final, splendid touch by studding the edges with brass upholstery nails.

This screen may look elaborate, but it's actually surprisingly easy to accomplish, and no difficult techniques or unusual equipment are needed.

MATERIALS AND EQUIPMENT

SHAPED PANELS
(SEE TEMPLATE ON PAGE 109)

BROWN VINYL MATT EMULSION
(FOR THE UNDERCOAT)

BROWN VINYL SILK EMULSION
(OR OTHER COLOUR AS PREFERRED)

STOUT, LONG-BRISTLED PAINTBRUSH

ACRYLIC GOLD SPRAY PAINT

RUBBER GLOVES

FACE MASK

UNWANTED LACE CURTAIN, OR LARGE
PIECE OF DAMASK LACE THE SIZE OF ONE
PANEL (1.8M X 0.6M/6FT X 2FT)

LOW-TACK SPRAY ADHESIVE
(E.G. SPRAY MOUNT)

ARTISTS' OIL COLOURS,
RAW AND BURNT UMBER

WHITE SPIRIT (TURPENTINE SUBSTITUTE)

SOFT CLOTH OR KITCHEN PAPER

OPTIONAL: 210 'ANTIQUE' BRASS OR BRASS-
PLATED UPHOLSTERY NAILS (70 PER PANEL)

BRADAWL

HAMMER

NOTE: various paints and solvents will be used for this project, so it is important to work in a well-ventilated area, and to protect your hands with rubber gloves. A face mask is recommended when using spray paint.

METHOD

1 Begin by priming each panel on both sides, and all edges, with one coat of brown emulsion paint. Vinyl matt emulsion is best, because matt paint gives a better key for the next coat. This priming coat prevents the next coat of paint soaking in, and so ensures it will be a truer colour. Check the paint is properly dry before going on to the next stage.

Applying the brown undercoat

2 Brown vinyl silk emulsion is used to create the leather effect. Coat the paintbrush liberally with the paint and really go to town, squidging the paint onto the surface with a circular movement. The aim is to achieve a random pattern of peaks and whorls, which will stand out in relief once the paint has dried. This is quite difficult to achieve while the paint is still wet, but if necessary you can go over it again with the same brush to sharpen up the pattern once it has started to dry.

Creating the leather effect

3 Once you have painted the front of each panel, leave the panels to dry overnight, then paint the back and edges of each one in the same way. They will take longer than the manufacturer's recommended drying time, because the emulsion has been applied so thickly.

Leave the second side to dry for at least 24 hours before proceeding to the next stage.

4 To simulate gold tooling on leather, gold paint is sprayed onto the painted surfaces through damask lace. Be sure to cover the surrounding area with newspaper, to avoid damage from drifting adhesive or paint, as you might not be able to remove unwanted paint later.

REMEMBER: it is important to follow the manufacturer's instructions when spraying adhesive and gold paint. Make sure your working area is well ventilated, and wear a mask to protect your face when spraying.

5 First, place the lace face down on newspaper. Spray the underside of the lace with low-tack adhesive, then carefully position it on one of the painted panels, making sure it covers it completely.

6 Next, spray the paint through the lace. Use plenty of paint, to ensure that the pattern is a rich, solid gold, and clearly defined.

Spraying gold paint through the lace

7 Allow the gold paint to dry (it shouldn't take long), then peel off the lace carefully. Repeat the process on both sides of each panel, then leave to dry completely.

8 The final stage is to 'antique' the panels, by toning down the surface and blending the colours together. This is achieved using artists' oil colours. Mix together small amounts of raw and burnt umber paint on an old plate, and put some white spirit (turpentine substitute) in a small container. Then, wearing rubber gloves, dip your fingers into the white spirit and then the paint, and smear the paint randomly onto the surface of the panels, rubbing well in. This process should accentuate the whorl patterns, but do not worry if the oil colour seems to obscure the gold patterning for the time being.

Rubbing in oil paint

9 Immediately rub off the excess paint, while it's still wet and rather tacky, using a soft cloth or kitchen paper. The aim is to absorb the paint on the raised areas of texture and reveal the gold once more, but do not rub too hard or for too long – just until the gold is visible. Allow these surfaces to dry, before treating the backs in the same way. Once both sides of the panels have been treated, leave them to dry thoroughly (this can take 2-3 days).

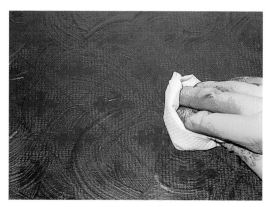

Rubbing off excess oil paint

It will help to prevent the panels splitting when you hammer in the studs, if you mark their position by piercing holes with a bradawl first.

10 If you want to give the screen a more authentic leather look, you can stud the top and side edges of each panel with 'antique' brass or brass-plated upholstery nails. First, mark the position of each stud by piercing a hole with a bradawl. Position the holes at regular intervals, say 6cm (2½in) apart, remembering to avoid the area where the hinges will go.

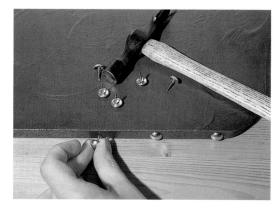

Studding the edges

11 Carefully tap the studs into the prepared holes, using the hammer.

12 Fit the hinges (see instructions on page 35), and your screen is complete.

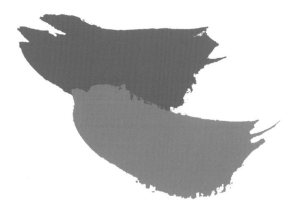

UPHOLSTERED SCREEN

The soft, upholstered look of this padded fabric screen can be achieved quickly and easily. You don't need specialist upholstery skills, and the materials and equipment used are very basic. It would look especially effective in a lounge or bedroom setting where its formal, luxurious style would enrich the surroundings. For a really integrated theme, you could use fabric that matches existing curtains and upholstery but, if you're feeling more adventurous, 'mix and match', and choose a new fabric that blends in well and complements your colour scheme.

If the fabric you choose has a very rigid pattern, remember that you will need more fabric than I have allowed. So, when buying the fabric, it is important to bear in mind the size of the pattern repeat in relation to the area of each panel, and ensure that you have enough material for the pattern to align on all three panels.

MATERIALS AND EQUIPMENT

SHAPED PANELS
(SEE TEMPLATE ON PAGE 110)

PLAIN OR RANDOMLY PATTERNED CURTAIN
OR UPHOLSTERY FABRIC, APPROX. 6.5M
(7YD) LENGTH, AT LEAST 137CM (54IN)
WIDE

110G (4OZ) POLYESTER WADDING: 5.5M
(6YD) LONG, BY AT LEAST 61CM (24IN) WIDE

BALLPOINT PEN/TAILOR'S CHALK

STAPLE GUN AND STAPLES

VERY SHARP SCISSORS

HOT MELT GLUE GUN OR
RUBBER SOLUTION GLUE

14M (15YD) CONTRASTING BRAID FOR
THE PANEL EDGES, AT LEAST 12MM (1/2IN)
WIDE.

NOTE: great care must be taken with hot melt glue, as it can burn the skin. If you use this type of glue, be sure to read the safety instructions before proceeding.

Take time to cut out the fabric as, once cut, it is difficult to compensate for a sloping pattern.

METHOD

1 Spread the fabric out, face down in a single layer, on a large flat surface with enough room to lay a screen panel lengthways on the fabric. You will be using only one half of the fabric width at this stage, as the other half will be used for the back of the panel.

2 Lay the panel on the fabric, 5cm (2in) in from the top and left edge of the fabric. This will allow enough additional fabric to fasten to the panel and wrap around the edges on those sides. Make sure the fabric pattern and grain are perfectly straight, as they must run vertically down the length of the panel when the screen is upright.

3 When you are sure the fabric is in line, use a ballpoint pen to mark the panel's position on the fabric. Next, remove the panel and use the ballpoint pen again to mark in the 5cm (2in) margins all around the marked outline of the panel. Cut out the fabric along the outer line.

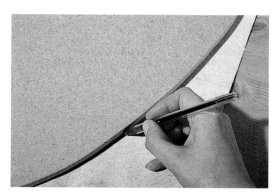

Marking out the fabric

4 Repeat this process along the other half width of the fabric, but this time, position the already cut piece and draw around that. Mark on the reverse side of the fabric which piece is for the front of the panel and which is for the back. Also mark on the top and the bottom to save any confusion later.

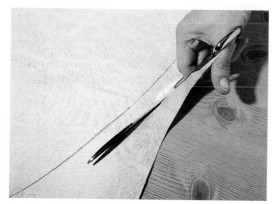

Cutting out the fabric

5 If the pattern repeats of your fabric need to align exactly on each panel, spread the remaining uncut fabric flat on the floor, patterned side up. Then position one of your already cut pieces on top of this fabric, also right side up, ensuring that the pattern on the cut piece aligns with the pattern on the remaining fabric. If you do not need to match your fabric then, obviously, you can repeat this process more quickly.

Use tailor's chalk instead of a pen to mark the patterned side of the fabric, as chalk can be removed more easily if you make a mistake.

---

6 Use the cut piece of fabric as a template, and draw around its edge – no need to allow extra margins this time, as they've already been included. Next, place the panel on the reverse side of the newly cut fabric, and draw round with a ballpoint pen to mark the margins. Repeat the process with the other cut piece on the matching half of the second width. Continue in this way until you have six cut pieces, each marked on the reverse, three identical ones for the front, and three for the back.

7 Take one of your back pieces and spread it out, wrong side facing up, on a large flat surface as before. Lay the screen panel on top of it, ensuring that the 5cm (2in) margin is evenly spaced all around.

Take care to keep the panel firmly in position on the fabric as you staple. It will spoil the run of the pattern on the other side if it shifts.

---

8 Then, starting with one of the long straight edges, lift the fabric up and over the edge of the panel and onto the other side, stapling each part as you go. The staples will, finally, need to be quite close together but, once the fabric has been anchored, you can always fill in the gaps with more staples later.

Stapling the back material to the panel

If you go wrong, you can remove the staples by lifting them with a small screwdriver and extracting them with pliers.

9 When you have completed one side, stretch the fabric tight and pull it up over the corresponding side, again stapling each area as you go along. It is important to stretch the fabric tightly across the panel to achieve a good finish.

10 When you've completed both long edges, begin across the top. If the top edge is curved, you will need to fold or pleat the fabric in order to accommodate the curve. Start in the middle of the top edge, pull the fabric over and anchor it with one staple. Repeat at each of the top corners, aiming to make each side of the centre staple the same. Continue by placing one staple between those already there, overlapping or pleating the fabric where necessary, and securing each pleat with a staple.

Continue along the bottom edge, taking especial care with the outer corners; for these you will need to fold the corner fabric inwards, to make a diagonal, before you pull the fabric onto the panel. Repeat on the other two panels.

11 When one side of each panel is covered, lay out the wadding on a flat surface and place the screen panel on top, with the material side uppermost. Use a marker pen to draw the panel shape onto the wadding, then remove the panel, and cut out the wadding shape. Repeat for the other two panels.

Marking out the wadding

12 Take one screen panel and, with the fabric-covered side face down, lay the wadding over the top, matching all the edges.

13 Secure the wadding on the panel by gluing along each side with a rubber solution glue. Apply liberally to the stapled fabric, close to the edge. Press the wadding down firmly and leave to dry. Repeat with the other two panels.

Sticking down the wadding

NOTE: The glue must be perfectly dry before proceeding with the next stage. If still wet, it will seep onto the other layer of fabric and spoil the effect.

14 When the glue has dried, take one of your front pieces of fabric and lay it over the top of the wadding, making sure it is positioned correctly and the pattern is straight.

It will be easier to staple the fabric to the front of the panel, if the panel is placed on a table top, wadding side up, with the edge to be worked on overhanging by a few inches. To keep the fabric in place while you staple, carefully pin the fabric to the wadding.

15 Once again, work along one long edge, holding the fabric down as you staple directly into the edge of the panel. Firmly secure one side with staples, then repeat along the other long side. Make sure the fabric is pulled fairly tight, but be careful to keep the tension even across the panel, or the fabric will look puckered.

Stapling the front fabric to the edge of the panel

16 Once both edges are secure, staple along the top and bottom. You may need to pleat the fabric along the top edge as before. Repeat with the other two panels.

17 Next, trim away the excess fabric. Place your first panel on a table top, making sure the side just covered is face down. Then, using sharp scissors, trim the fabric as close to the staples as you can, so that you leave a neat edge. Repeat on the other two panels.

Cutting off excess fabric

18 To finish all the edges, cover the staples with braid. With the panel still flat on a table, glue the braid into place using either a hot melt glue gun or a rubber solution glue. First, turn under the loose end of braid, and glue the panel edge, bit by bit, sticking down the braid as you go. Continue right around the panel, making sure the braid is in line with the edges. Neaten any subsequent ends of braid in the same way, by folding them under and gluing them down. Repeat on the other two panels.

Gluing braid onto the edges

19 When each panel edge has been covered you can attach the hinges and your screen will be complete.

For detailed instructions on attaching hinges, see 'How to Make a Solid Panel Screen' (page 35).

DRIFTWOOD SCREEN
with shell decoration

Allow 3–4 days to complete

This screen emulates the wonderful, weathered look of driftwood, mellowed by the tide and bleached by the sun. The seaside theme is followed through with starfish patterns on each panel, created out of shells, some decorated with metallicised colours, to evoke the lustrous sheen of mother-of-pearl.

The screen is quick and inexpensive to make, uses no specialised equipment or difficult techniques, and its simple decoration and neutral tones make it perfect for a bathroom. If you don't already have suitable shells to decorate your screen, you now have an excellent excuse to go to the beach and find some!

If you choose to follow my starfish design, bear in mind that you'll need a large centre shell for each panel, five large shells to position around it, to mark the points of the star, and shells graded from large to small for the rays of the starfish. Sort the shells into groups, before you begin painting them, so that you have roughly the same mixture of shells on each panel. Select as many interesting and varied shapes as you can find, but bear in mind that the flatter ones are best, as they are less likely to be knocked or damaged once the screen is in use.

MATERIALS AND EQUIPMENT

SHAPED PANELS
(SEE TEMPLATE ON PAGE 111)

BRILLIANT WHITE MATT EMULSION

FINE GRADE WIRE WOOL

DARK BROWN LIQUID FURNITURE WAX

RUBBER GLOVES
(not shown in photographs)

ASSORTMENT OF SEASHELLS

METALLIC PAINTS: GREEN, BLUE
AND SILVER

HOT MELT GLUE GUN OR STRONG,
ALL-PURPOSE CLEAR ADHESIVE

ARTISTS' BRUSH (MEDIUM SIZE)

IMITATION SILVER LEAF

SIZE TO STICK THE SILVER LEAF TO
THE SURFACE

SOFT CLOTH OR KITCHEN PAPER

CLEAR ACRYLIC VARNISH

NOTE: great care must be taken with hot melt glue, as it can burn the skin. If you use this type of glue, be sure to read the safety instructions before proceeding.

METHOD

1 Paint both sides of each panel with the white emulsion. Don't worry if the brush strokes make the panels look a little streaky, this will add to the desired effect, but be careful you don't brush the paint out too thinly, as some of it will be removed during the next stage. Leave the panels to dry overnight.

Undercoating the panels

2 Once the panels are completely dry, you can apply the coloured wax. This enhances the driftwood effect, by smoothing the painted surface, and leaves each panel with a silky smooth sheen. First, put on rubber gloves – these will protect your fingers from the harsh wire wool, and your hands from staining by the coloured wax. Apply wax to the wool, and rub it into the paint in the direction of the grain – i.e. from top to bottom – so that it darkens the paint, and gives a streaky effect. Continue in this way until all the surfaces of each panel are treated. You can then decorate the fronts of the panels with the shells.

If the wax is slow to come out of the tin, warm it a little, by standing the tin in a bowl of warm water for a while and then shaking it thoroughly. If it's still too thick, leave it in the water a little longer, and try again.

Waxing the panels

3 If you like a natural look, place the shells straight on the panel, without embellishment; if you prefer to add a little colour, do as I have done, and enhance some of the shells with metallic paint. Using a medium artists' brush, paint a few of the shells with the green metallic paint – it's up to you whether you paint the whole of the shells, just patches of colour, or a combination of the two. Experiment to see which you prefer. I've even painted a mixture of colours on some shells, but left others unpainted.

4 When you've painted some shells with the green, you can paint others with the blue and silver metallic paint. Leave the shells to dry thoroughly before gluing them to the screen.

Painting the shells with metallic paint

5 Next, mark the centre of the panels. Lay the panels out flat, and measure halfway lines from top to bottom, and then side to side; mark the centre point where the two lines cross.

6 Lay out the shells you've selected for a panel, and place one of the larger shells on the centre point. Next, position five large shells around it, to mark the points of the star, then add more shells along the points, grading them from large to small as you go. Once you are happy with the points of the rays, add more shells to make up the body of the starfish, and make the points of the rays wider nearer the ends. Decorate the other two panels in the same way, making sure the designs will look balanced when the screen is completed.

If you're using a glue gun, remember to warm it before use and work quickly as once the glue has cooled down, it will become hard and the shells won't stick.
If using clear adhesive, instead of the glue gun, use it sparingly, or it may ooze from behind the shells, leaving a messy finish. Also, clear adhesive takes longer to dry, so it's best to leave the panels laid out flat while the glue dries.

7 Once you're happy with the design, glue the shells onto the panels. Work on one shell at a time, carefully placing a thin line of glue around the underside rim, and repositioning it on the panel before gluing the next shell. Continue until all the shells are stuck firmly in position on the three panels, then leave them to dry thoroughly, before adding the finishing touches.

Sticking on the shells

8 Once all the shells are stuck down firmly, you can decorate the panels with silver wiggly lines, to continue the theme of driftwood. First apply the size for the silver leaf. Take a medium artists' brush, and paint random, uneven, wiggly lines of size all over one of the panels. The lines should be vertical, approximately 15–20cm (6–8in) long, spaced out over the body of the panel, but radiated up from the bottom edge. Once you have completed one panel, allow approximately 15 minutes for the size to dry, before applying the silver leaf.

Painting on the size for the silver decoration

Work on just one panel at a time; the size used to fix the silver leaf dries quickly, so you won't have time to apply the silver to all three panels in one go.

9 The size is ready when it has become tacky, and the colour has changed from milky-white to clear. Once this happens, take a sheet of silver leaf, along with its backing paper, and lay it silver-side down on a sized area. Use a soft paintbrush to gently brush over the backing paper then, once the silver has adhered to the panel, remove the paper.

Applying the silver leaf

Leave the panels flat out while you apply the silver leaf, so you can collect the loose flakes for re-use later.

10 Use your fingers to gently pull away any excess silver leaf; this excess leaf can be saved for use on another area. Then gently rub over the silver leaf just applied, with a piece of kitchen paper or soft cloth, to remove any small excess flakes. These too can be gathered up and re-used. Once the three panels are complete, you can apply the varnish.

Rubbing off excess silver leaf

11 To protect the silver leaf, and prevent it tarnishing, coat the front of each panel with at least two layers of hard-wearing acrylic varnish. The varnish will dry clear, and give a lustrous sheen that brings out the colour of both the natural and the painted shells.

Varnishing the panels

12 Once the varnish is dry, the hinges can be attached (see detailed instructions on page 35) and your screen is complete.

MUSIC SCORE SCREEN

Allow 3–4 days to complete

This richly decorated and embellished screen, with its gold leaf details and old script, would look at home in any dining room or study, or even the music room itself. The flowing curves of the two outer panels are inspired by the old music stands that used to stand in the corner of period homes, while the aged copies of music scores allude to the manuscripts that would have rested on them.

If you haven't got any music scores, don't worry, as they can often be found in libraries or charity shops. Look for scores with interesting text or script – or even illustrations – as well as the music itself, as this will make the finished result more varied and pleasing. So that the original scores are preserved intact, photocopy them, enlarging or reducing them if you wish, to suit your requirements. Separate them into three piles, one for each panel, and, once you have all the photocopies you need, they can be 'aged' (see overleaf), using ordinary tea and instant coffee.

Although the screen shown here is made from elaborately cut and shaped panels, it is easily possible to re-create the same feel on standard pre-cut panels, with little specialised equipment or difficult techniques.

MATERIALS AND EQUIPMENT

PREPARED PANELS
(SEE TEMPLATE ON PAGE 112)

BURGUNDY VINYL SILK EMULSION

MEDIUM AND FINE GRADE SANDPAPER

PHOTOCOPIES OF OLD MUSIC SCORES

ORDINARY TEA BAGS AND COFFEE
GRANULES FOR 'AGEING' THE SCORES

OLD NEWSPAPERS

BLU-TACK

PVA GLUE AND GLUE SPATULA

ANTIQUE GOLD POSTER PAINT

IMITATION GOLD LEAF SHEETS

GOLD LEAF SIZE (TO STICK THE GOLD
LEAF TO THE PANELS)

SOFT PAINTBRUSH

SOFT CLOTH OR KITCHEN PAPER

CHALK

LIQUID GOLD LEAF

TURPENTINE

ARTISTS' BRUSHES, INCLUDING FLAT-ENDED

GILDING CREAM (E.G. 'TREASURE GOLD')

CLEAR SATIN ACRYLIC VARNISH

MALT VINEGAR

METHOD

1 Using a medium-sized decorators' brush, undercoat your three screen panels all over with the burgundy emulsion paint. Allow the first side to dry for 3–4 hours, paint the reverse side, then leave the panels to dry overnight.

Undercoating the panels

Be careful you don't overload the brush, as this will cause the paint to drip and run, and spoil the finished result.

---

2 While the panels are drying, you can 'age' your photocopied music scores. First, make some very strong tea, with at least three tea bags; stir well, then leave the tea to cool. Place the photocopied sheets flat on top of several thicknesses of newspaper, so that any excess liquid will be soaked up.

'Ageing' photocopies with cold tea

3 Once the tea is cool, take one of the tea bags – being careful not to squeeze out too much liquid – and wipe the surface of each photocopied page liberally with it, until the paper begins to take on a yellowish tint. If the tea bag bursts, don't worry; just continue with one of the others, until all your photocopies have been treated.

You can, if necessary, keep re-dipping your tea bag into the tea, so you have enough liquid to cover all your pages.

4 While the paper is still wet, take a few instant coffee granules and sprinkle them over the wet pages in small patches. This is to simulate the brown speckles often found on old manuscripts that have been stored for a long time. Allow the granules to soak into the paper, and leave the pages to dry completely.

'Ageing' photocopies with coffee granules

5 Next day, when the painted panels are dry, you will find the paint has raised the grain of the MDF, so you'll need to sand the panels until smooth to the touch. First, rub the paint back a little, using the medium grade sandpaper. Take great care you don't rub too hard: the bare MDF should not become visible through the paint, although, if the paint looks a little streaky after sanding, that will add to the overall 'aged' effect. Finish off the process with the finer grade paper, to give a silky smooth texture.

Pay special attention to the panel edges, as these usually require the most sanding to become smooth.

6 Once the pages are dry, you can decorate the panels. First, choose the most detailed or interesting areas from some of the larger pages. Tear out these selected areas, in fairly rough pieces – squares, rectangles or just random pieces, it's entirely up to you – then arrange them on your panels. Treat all the other photocopies in the same way.

Tearing the photocopies

It's much easier to judge the arrangement of the pieces if you stand the panels up, and position the torn pieces using Blu-Tack. In this way you can try out an arrangement, check that the design on the three panels will be balanced, and reposition the pieces as necessary.

7 If you like, you can add still more interest to the panels by applying areas of antique gold poster paint in rough squares underneath the pieces, before you stick them down. When the paint is dry, and you are satisfied with the design, the pieces can be glued in place.

Painting gold under the photocopies

It is much easier to paint on the patches of gold if you use an artists' flat-ended acrylic brush; this will give wide, even brush strokes, but remember all your brush strokes must go in one direction for a neat effect.

8 Remove one image from the design at a time, and take off the Blu-Tack. Place the image face down on scrap paper and apply the glue. Start gluing from the middle of the sheet, and work carefully out towards the edges.

Once the paper is coated liberally with glue, press the image firmly back in position on the panel.

When all the pieces are fixed in position, go over the edges of each torn piece with the gold poster paint; if you wish, you can also paint random patches of gold on other areas of the panels.

Gluing the photocopies

Sheets of gold leaf are paper thin, and must be handled with great care. It is easier to decide where to position each piece while the panels are still upright, but the gold leaf itself is easier to fix on with the panels laid flat.

9 You can now embellish the panels with the imitation gold leaf sheets. First, carefully select the areas where you want gold leaf. You can apply square patches, as I have done here, or apply more randomly, perhaps overlapping the manuscript pieces, or areas you have painted gold. Be adventurous! Use a small brush to paint size on a few areas at a time, then leave the size to dry for about 15 minutes.

Applying size for the gold leaf

It is important to apply the size to small areas at a time, as it's quite difficult to see the size once it has dried.

10 When the size changes colour, from a milky-white to clear, it's time to apply the gold leaf. Don't attempt to apply the leaf before this, as the size would smear over the surface, and leave an untidy edge.

Fixing the gold leaf

11 Very carefully remove one sheet of gold leaf from the packaging, with its tissue paper backing intact. Gently lay it, gold side down, on a sized area and, with a very soft paintbrush, gently rub over the backing paper to adhere the leaf to the size. Remove the backing paper and, with a piece of kitchen paper or soft cloth, carefully rub over the surface and edges of the leaf very carefully to remove any excess gold. Repeat the process on the other sized areas, until you are happy with all three panels.

Rubbing off excess gold leaf

Save any large pieces of leaf that are rubbed away, and apply to other areas in due course.

12 Once all the gold leaf is in place, you may add more details with liquid leaf. This is especially useful for adding areas of text, single words, or other musical terms and expressions which you may copy from your old music scores. Decide where you want these to go and, with a piece of ordinary blackboard chalk, write or draw them on the panels. Continue over the whole of each panel until you are pleased with the results.

Marking on patterns with chalk

If you make mistakes with your chalk marks, you can always rub them out with a piece of kitchen paper, and do them again.

Liquid leaf comes in a small bottle and, on standing, separates out. Mix it well before use, to distribute the metallic particles evenly throughout the base. The brush can be cleaned after use with turpentine.

13 Next, give the liquid gold leaf a good shake or stir. Dip the fine artists' brush into the liquid leaf and paint it over your chalk marks. Once you have completed all the panels, allow the gold leaf to dry overnight before attempting to rub out any remaining chalk marks.

Painting liquid leaf over the chalk patterns

14 For a finishing touch, you can, if you wish, gild the edges of each panel with gilding cream. To do this, apply a small amount of cream along all the edges using your fingertip. This is surprisingly easy and effective to do and gives each panel a neat, gilded edge.

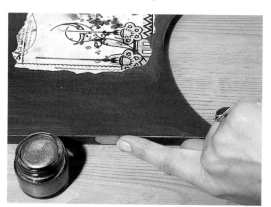

Gilding the panel edges

15 When you have completed the surface decoration, coat both sides of each panel with two layers of hard-wearing clear satin acrylic varnish. Be sure to follow the manufacturers' recommendations for drying times, and allow the first coat to dry before applying the second one.

Varnishing the panels

16 Once the varnish is dry, you can attach the hinges (see instructions on page 35), and your screen is complete.

If you feel the brass hinges are too shiny, place them in a small container and cover them with ordinary malt vinegar. This will remove the surface shine, and give the hinges an 'aged' look. Leave the hinges to soak overnight, or until they tarnish, then wash them in warm water and dry them thoroughly before attaching to your screen.

DECOUPAGE SCREEN
with crackle background

Allow 3–4 days to complete

Decoupage was the height of fashion in Victorian times. Victorian ladies loved elaborate and detailed decoration, and would spend hours cutting out small photographs and images saved from greetings cards and scrapbooks. These were pasted onto hat boxes, jewellery cases and decorative screens and, once completely covered, these lovingly created pieces were varnished to protect their delicate surfaces from wear. Many of these pieces survive in almost mint condition, with just a slightly yellowed or cracked varnish to show their age.

My screen is inspired by the Victorian technique but, instead of covering the entire surface with cut images, I have given the screen panels a background of crackle paint, which adds interest, colour and texture.

Decoupage 'scraps' can be bought from craft shops, but you may prefer to collect your own. If you want the same images on each panel, photocopy them twice, using a colour photocopier, enlarging or reducing them if you wish. Fit as many images as you can onto blank sheets of A4 paper, and fix them in place with tiny pieces of Blu-Tack, so that they can be detached easily after photocopying. When you have enough to create the desired effect, cut out the photocopied images and separate them into three piles, one for each panel.

MATERIALS AND EQUIPMENT

SHAPED PANELS
(SEE TEMPLATE ON PAGE 113)

PALE BLUE VINYL SILK EMULSION
(UNDERCOAT FOR PANEL BACKS AND
EDGES, AND TOP COAT FOR PANEL FRONTS)

DARK BLUE VINYL SILK EMULSION
(UNDERCOAT FOR PANEL FRONTS)

5CM (2IN) DECORATORS' BRUSH

MEDIUM AND FINE GRADE SANDPAPER

MASKING TAPE (OPTIONAL)

CRACKLE MEDIUM

SHARP SCISSORS

BOUGHT SCRAPS, OR IMAGES CUT FROM
MAGAZINES, COLOURED PHOTOCOPIES, ETC
FOR THE DECOUPAGE

BLU-TACK

PVA GLUE

GLUE SPREADER

BROWN UMBER ARTISTS' OIL PAINT

CLEAR SATIN POLYURETHANE VARNISH
(APPROX. 300ML, OR HALF A TIN)

NOTE: if you use an oil-based varnish, such as polyurethane, you must tint it with an oil-based paint. If you use an acrylic varnish, you must tint it with an acrylic paint. The two are not interchangeable, so take care that you have the correct combination.

METHOD

1 Undercoat the edges and backs of each screen panel with the pale blue emulsion and leave to dry overnight.

2 Undercoat the front of each panel with the dark blue emulsion paint and leave to dry overnight.

Painting the undercoat for the crackle medium

Before trying out the crackle technique on the real thing, practise on a small offcut of MDF as it takes confidence and a little practice to obtain a good result. The same offcut can be used to test the tinted varnish applied at the end.

To highlight the crackled surface, use contrasting colours of paint. This will ensure the underneath layer of paint shows through when the top coat crackles.

3 Once the undercoated surfaces are completely dry, you may find the paint has raised the texture of the MDF slightly, making it rough to the touch. If so, sand all the surfaces back a little by hand, paying particular attention to the edges. Begin by sanding gently with the medium-grade sandpaper until the surface feels smooth to the touch, then sand with the finer grade, until the surface has a silky smooth feel.

To protect the panel fronts from unwelcome paint splashes, place masking tape along the front edges, before applying the top coat of pale emulsion to the sides and backs. The panel edges can be protected in the same way, when applying the crackle medium to the fronts of the panels (see stage 5).

4 Apply a second, top coat of pale blue emulsion to the edges and backs of the panels, making sure the paint does not drip onto the front. Allow to dry, as before.

In order for the top layer of paint to crack, crackle medium is applied to the front of the panels between two layers of emulsion paint. This causes the top layer of paint to shrink and split, exposing the undercoat in the cracks. Applying the final layer of paint over the crackle medium takes time and much concentration, so work on just one panel at a time at this stage, to ensure the result is not spoilt by hurrying.

5 Use a medium-size decorators' paintbrush to apply the crackle medium to the front of the screen, over the dark blue paint. Do not overload the brush, as this will cause the medium to drip and spoil the final effect.

Applying the crackle medium

To ensure the maximum amount of cracking, it is important that the brush strokes of the crackle medium are at right angles to the subsequent brush strokes of the final layer of emulsion, so work methodically down the length of the screen in straight lines, from top to bottom. Continue in this way until the whole of the panel is completely covered with the crackle medium.

6 Leave the crackle medium to dry for 15–20 minutes, or until it changes colour from a milky-white to clear. When it is ready to work over, the surface will feel slightly tacky and it's important that you continue immediately with the next stages. If the crackle medium becomes too dry, it will prevent the cracks from forming later.

7 While the crackle is drying, wash the paintbrush with water, ready for use with the final layer of paint.

8 As soon as the crackle medium has cleared, apply the top coat of paint. Load the brush well with the pale blue emulsion and, working from left to right, smooth the paint over the crackle medium. Work in one direction only, and keep the line of the brush as straight as possible.

Painting over the crackle medium

Do not attempt to go back over the area you have just painted, as this will cause the paint to lift off from the surface, pulling the crackle medium with it and creating a rough lumpy effect devoid of any cracks. You will have to keep re-loading the brush to cover such a large area, but make sure that one brush stroke follows on into the next as smoothly as possible, so that you are not left with uneven patches. Also, make sure that the last line of paint just touches the line above but does not overlap, as this, too, would cause a raised texture on the surface.

9 If you find you have missed some areas, leave them until last and then fill in the gaps in the same way; work in one direction only this time, using a small artists' brush. Do not attempt to fill in missed areas with a larger brush, as it would ruin the effect.

10 When the whole of the panel front has been painted, repeat the process on the fronts of the other two panels. Leave each one to dry completely before continuing with the next stage. The cracks should begin to appear almost immediately and get larger as the paint dries.

11 Once the paint is completely dry, you can apply the decoupage detail over the crackled surface. If you stand your first screen panel in an upright position, it will make it easier to arrange the images in a pleasing design. Again, use a little Blu-Tack to attach the images to the panel, so that you can re-arrange them easily. When you are happy with the design, line up the other two panels, so that you can check as you go that the pictures are aligned on all three panels.

Cutting out the pictures

Arranging the decoupage

12 When you are satisfied with the whole design, remove the Blu-Tack from one image at a time, and spread PVA glue liberally on the reverse of the image. Carefully reposition the images, ensuring that the edges are stuck down well. Complete all three panels, then leave the glue to dry overnight.

Applying glue to the decoupage pieces

13 If you wish to 'age' the screen, you can tint the polyurethane varnish with brown umber artists' oil paint. Half a tin of varnish (approx. 300ml) should be ample to cover the three panels with one coat of varnish, so double the quantity if you want to apply two coats. Add half a teaspoon of paint to the varnish and mix well; if you want a slightly darker tint, add a little more paint, very gradually, until you are happy with the colour.

Before applying the tinted varnish to the screen, test the colour on the MDF offcut you used for experimenting with the crackle medium.

14 Once the colour is right, varnish both sides and edges of each panel. If you want to apply a second coat, be sure to allow time in between coats for the varnish to dry thoroughly.

Varnishing the panels

The decoration is now complete, and you can attach the hinges to your screen (see detailed instructions on page 35).

WALLPAPERED SCREEN
with ornamental shield

Allow 4–5 days to complete

This is an impressive screen, richly decorated, and 'aged' to simulate cracked and yellowing varnish. The gilded ornamental shield echoes the heraldic theme of the fleur-de-lis wallpaper, giving the screen an air of pageantry suitable for a more formal area of the home, such as the lounge, dining room or study.

There are many ready-made ornaments available which could be used to decorate the front of your screen; these range from plaster casts to carved wooden pieces, and they can be used as they are or, for a more imposing effect, gilded like mine.

I have chosen to paint the backs of my panels, but you might prefer to wallpaper both sides. If so, remember to double the amount of wallpaper allowed, and to follow the same processes as described for the fronts of the panels.

For a more co-ordinated look, you could match your screen to wallpaper already existing in the chosen room, perhaps using up roll ends.

MATERIALS AND EQUIPMENT

SHAPED PANELS
(SEE TEMPLATE ON PAGE 114)

WALLPAPER PASTE

LARGE PASTE BRUSH

SATIN EMULSION PAINT FOR PANEL BACKS
AND SIDES, TO MATCH COLOUR IN
WALLPAPER

MEDIUM AND FINE GRADE SANDPAPER

2 ROLLS OF WALLPAPER (OR ENOUGH ROLL
ENDS TO COVER ONE SIDE OF EACH
SCREEN PANEL)

SOFT CLOTH OR KITCHEN PAPER

SHARP SCISSORS

PVA GLUE AND GLUE SPATULA

SHARP CRAFT KNIFE (OPTIONAL)

CRACKLE VARNISH

CRACKLE GLAZE

MEDIUM-SIZE PAINTBRUSH

BURNT UMBER ARTISTS' ACRYLIC PAINT

ORNAMENT/S TO DECORATE THE SCREEN
(GILDED OR PLAIN)

OPTIONAL: COLOURED CORD AND TASSELS
TO MATCH OR CONTRAST WITH THE
WALLPAPER

14M (15YD) BRAID TO FINISH THE EDGES

HOT MELT GLUE GUN OR ALL-PURPOSE
CLEAR ADHESIVE AND GLUE SPREADER

*NOTE: if you choose to gild your ornament,
you will also need red emulsion paint;
acrylic gold size; imitation gold leaf and
clear satin acrylic varnish.*

METHOD

1 First you need to size the front of each panel with a preliminary layer of wallpaper paste. This will prevent the next coat of paste, for the wallpaper itself, soaking into the MDF, and make it easier to stick the paper evenly to the surface. Mix approximately 0.25 litre (¹/₂pt) wallpaper paste to a medium thick consistency according to the instructions on the packet. Then, using a large brush, size one side of each screen panel thoroughly with the paste. Leave the panels to dry.

2 Next, undercoat the back of each panel with the satin emulsion paint. Allow to dry, then sand down, first with the medium grade sandpaper, then with the fine grade. The final coat of paint is added at a later stage.

3 Now cut a length of wallpaper for the central panel. To calculate the amount of wallpaper you need, measure the longest length of the panel, and add on 20cm (8in). Only cut this one length of wallpaper at this stage. The paper will not be wide enough to cover the whole front of the panel, so you will need to cut fill-in strips to go either side at a later stage, after the centre piece has been stuck down.

4 Mix approximately 0.5 litre (1pt) paste, according to the instructions on the packet. Lay the cut length of wallpaper face down, and apply a generous coat of paste to the back. Start pasting in the centre, then continue pasting from the centre out, towards the edges. Be sure to cover the entire sheet with paste, paying special attention to the edges. Once pasted, loosely fold the two ends of the wallpaper towards the centre, so that the pasted sides are together in concertina-type folds. Try not to get paste on the front of the wallpaper, as it would have to be removed with a damp cloth later.

5 Lay one of the panels out flat, pre-sized side uppermost. Place the pasted wallpaper on the panel, with the folded ends underneath, then gently open out the two folded ends so the paper is flat. Carefully manoeuvre the wallpaper into position, until you are sure it is centred on the panel, and straight.

complete width of wallpaper

match pattern here

2 half widths to fill sides

spare paper to be trimmed

6 Once you are happy with the placing of the wallpaper, you can gently smooth it, pressing over the surface with a soft folded cloth. Start smoothing in the centre, and work out towards the edges, aiming to remove air bubbles, and flatten the paper. Leave the panel to dry.

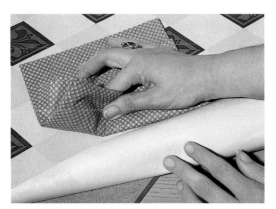

Smoothing the wallpaper with a soft cloth

If, in spite of your best endeavours, large air pockets do appear in the centre, you can lift the wallpaper; peel it back, either from the top or the bottom (but definitely not from the side edge, as this might tear it) and gently lay the paper back down again, smoothing out the air pockets as you go.

---

7 If you are using patterned wallpaper, it is important that the patterns on the fill-in pieces, either side of the piece already stuck down, align. To ensure this, unroll the remaining length of wallpaper alongside the central panel; adjust the roll of paper by moving it upwards, until the patterns match at the edges. Once the patterns align, mark the length, and add on at least a 10cm (4in) excess at the bottom, before cutting off the length from the roll. This piece will be sufficient for both fill-in pieces for the one panel. Divide the measured length in two, this time by folding it from top to bottom down a central line. Cut along the fold, so that you are left with two halves of one length.

8 Decide which piece of wallpaper is for the left side of the panel, and which for the right, and paste up one piece on the reverse, following the procedure as before. Position the chosen side piece of wallpaper alongside the central stuck-down piece, making sure the patterns align. Once you are happy, stick this piece down. Repeat the process with the other side piece, and then wallpaper the other two panels in the same way.

Allow the panels to dry completely before attempting the next stage. If the paper is still wet (and therefore soft), it may rip or tear, which would spoil all your hard work.

9 Once the wallpaper is dry, work on the centre panel, with the wallpapered side uppermost. Trim off the excess paper from the edges, using sharp scissors, leaving a margin of approximately 2.5cm (1in) all around. It doesn't have to be measured accurately, but make sure you leave sufficient excess paper to glue over the sides and hide the edges of the panel.

Cutting off excess paper

If possible, position the panel over a table top, so that it overhangs by a few inches. It will then be easier to trim the excess paper, and snip into the edges, without being hampered by the table top.

10 Next, make snips in the excess paper, around all the edges. Snip at right angles to the panel, and at 1cm (³⁄₈in) intervals; this will make it easier to turn the wallpaper over the edges, and is especially necessary if the screen panel curves.

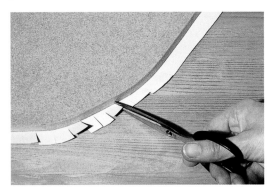

Snipping the edges

11 Now glue the snipped paper over the edges of the panel. Use PVA glue because, in some areas, one layer of paper will need to be stuck on top of another, and wallpaper paste is not a strong enough adhesive to do this effectively. Begin by smearing the PVA liberally onto the back of the snipped edges, using a glue spatula or similar device, and stick down each piece as you go. Be especially careful to pull the paper tight around the curves, gluing one snipped piece on top of the other, and over the edges, aiming to prevent air pockets forming, and retain a neat edge. Continue until all the edges have been covered, then repeat on the other two panels. Leave to dry completely before the next stage.

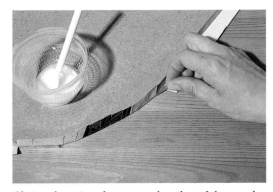

Gluing the snipped paper to the edge of the panel

12 Once the glue has dried, trim off any excess paper with scissors (see photograph). Repeat on the other two panels.

Trimming the edges

13 Apply the second, top coat, of satin emulsion paint to the backs of the panels, and leave to dry before the next stage.

Applying the crackle varnish can be a tricky operation. There are no second chances and you cannot go back over the area that you have just covered; if you do, the varnish underneath will lift, causing raised rough patches which will ruin the overall effect. If you are at all unsure about the process, it is a good idea to practise on another surface first.

---

14 Once wallpapered, the fronts of the panels may be varnished. First, mix together equal parts of crackle varnish and crackle glaze – about 1/2 cup of each – in an old container. With the screen panel upright, use a medium-sized paintbrush to apply the varnish and glaze mixture to the wallpapered surface. Begin at the top of the panel, and work from the top down, painting on the mixture with even brush strokes. When you have applied one layer to each panel, leave them to dry for at least two hours.

Applying the crackle varnish and glaze undercoat

Take care not to overload the brush with the mixture, as this will cause drips, but do not brush it out too thinly, either; try to keep the coat as even as possible, and make sure that the brush strokes are in one direction only.

---

15 When the first varnish coat is completely dry, apply another layer of the varnish and glaze mixture, brushing from top to bottom as before, and leave the panels to dry once again.

Cover the container for the crackle varnish and glaze mixture with clingfilm between use, to seal it and prevent the mixture drying out.

---

16 For the final layer, use crackle varnish on its own; this will cause the cracks to appear, so it is vital that you follow the instructions carefully. Beginning at the top of the centre panel, brush on the varnish from left to right (i.e. at right angles to the two undercoats of varnish and glaze mixture). To ensure the surface crackles evenly, it is essential that you only paint over each area once, and that you keep the lines of varnish horizontal; if the brush strokes begin to slope, it will be very noticeable on the finished panel. Cracks will appear as the varnish dries. When you've covered the three panels in this way, leave them to dry overnight before continuing.

Applying acrylic paint to the cracks

18 You can now add the finishing touches. If you choose to gild an unpainted, ready-made ornament, first check to see if it has a surface finish, such as varnish; if so, sand it down with fine sandpaper to give it a good key for painting. Next, undercoat it with emulsion. Traditionally, this undercoat would have been red oxide in colour, but I have used a vivid red emulsion paint which gives similar results and is easier to obtain. Give each ornament one even coat of paint, then leave to dry.

Applying the crackle varnish top coat

17 Once the varnish is completely dry, gently rub some burnt umber acrylic paint into the cracks. Put a little of the neat paint on a soft cloth or kitchen paper, and apply to small areas of the panel at first, then gradually work over the whole surface. Rub the paint in gently, using circular movements, to ensure it becomes well embedded into the cracks. You may need to dip the cloth into some water at intervals, to make the paint flow more easily over the surface, but it is important not to use too much water, as this will wash the paint off altogether.

Obviously, the more paint you apply, the darker the resulting surface colour, but be careful not to obliterate the wallpaper pattern. Repeat the process on the other two panels, and leave to dry once again.

19 Once the paint has dried, use a flat-ended brush to coat the painted ornament with an even layer of acrylic gold size. The size is milky-white in appearance on application but, once it is ready to work with, it becomes clear. When the size becomes tacky, about 15 minutes after application, stick down the gold leaf.

20 Take a sheet of gold leaf, along with its tissue paper backing, and lay the sheet gold side down on the ornament. Using a soft paintbrush, smooth down the gold leaf through the tissue paper, until it is stuck to the surface. Remove the backing and then, with a soft cloth or sheet of kitchen paper, rub over the gold leaf to remove any excess flakes. These can be collected and used again later. Continue in this way until the whole of the ornament is covered in gold leaf. Do not worry if there are gaps where the paint shows through – these will add to the overall 'aged' effect of the piece.

21 If you wish to 'age' the ornament further, you can darken the gold leaf slightly by gently rubbing a little neat dark brown acrylic paint into the surface, using a soft cloth or kitchen paper. When you are satisfied with the results, leave the paint to dry.

22 Once the paint is dry, coat the ornament with two layers of clear satin acrylic varnish, following the manufacturer's advice about drying times between layers. The varnish will protect the piece, and prevent the gold leaf tarnishing over time.

NOTE: if using a hot melt glue gun, be extremely careful. The hot glue can burn if it comes into contact with skin.

23 Once the varnish is dry, decide where you want to place the ornament on the centre panel, and mark the position. Lay the panel out flat, with the wallpapered side uppermost. Then, using either the hot melt glue gun, or a strong, clear all-purpose adhesive, spread glue liberally over the back of the ornament and stick it firmly in place. Do not stand the panel up until the glue is dry. If you have ornaments on the side panels as well, treat in the same way, and make sure they align with the centre panel.

Applying adhesive to the ornament with a spreader

Sticking down the ornament

24 If you wish, you can embellish the panels further with contrasting lengths of cord and tassels. Glue these into position with the glue gun or adhesive as before.

Arranging the cord detail (optional)

25 To finish off the panels, glue – using the glue gun or rubber solution glue – matching or contrasting braid around the edges. Turn under the loose end of braid and, starting at a bottom left edge, stick it firmly down. Continue round the panel, gluing a section of the panel edge at a time, carefully positioning the braid, and sticking it down as you go. Turn under the final end of braid, as before, and glue it down to give a neat finish.

26 Once each panel edge has been covered, you can attach the hinges (see instructions on page 35). Your screen is then complete.

VERDIGRIS SCREEN
with papier-mâché detail

While out walking in public parks or gardens, you may have noticed bronze statues that have been weathered by the elements, and are no longer the rich colour that they once were. This is because the outdoor weather conditions have attacked the surface of the metal, transforming it with a multitude of subtle shades of pale powdery greens and blues into the wonderful hue known as verdigris.

With this screen, I have used various paint effects to capture the patina of verdigris, and have added interest, with raised papier-mâché details of twining plants, highlighted with bronze liquid leaf paint.

The paper for the papier-mâché pulp could be newspaper, which you can shred by hand, or paper that has already been through an office shredder, if you are lucky enough to have access to one. Bear in mind that you need to allow at least two days for the paper to soak and soften, and possibly several additional days for the papier-mâché details to dry on the panels, but this is a charming screen and well worth the wait.

MATERIALS AND EQUIPMENT

SHAPED PANELS, WITH PRE-MARKED DESIGN (SEE TEMPLATE ON PAGE 115)

2 WHOLE BROADSHEET NEWSPAPERS, SHREDDED FOR PAPIER-MACHE PULP

OLD, LARGE, HEAVY-BOTTOMED SAUCEPAN

SIEVE

OLD POTATO MASHER

WALLPAPER PASTE

TIN OF COPPER PAINT, WITH HAMMERED METAL FINISH

OLD PAINTBRUSH TO APPLY THE COPPER PAINT

SOLVENT FOR COPPER PAINT (AS RECOMMENDED BY MANUFACTURER)

PALE BLUE SATIN EMULSION PAINT

GREEN SATIN EMULSION PAINT

STIPPLING BRUSH

FINE GRADE SANDPAPER

ARTISTS' ACRYLIC PAINT SHADES: PTHALO GREEN AND PTHALO BLUE

MEDIUM AND FINE ARTISTS' BRUSHES

BRONZE LIQUID LEAF

TURPENTINE

ACRYLIC SATIN VARNISH

METHOD

1 First, finely shred the paper for the papier-mâché. If you are shredding it by hand, tear it lengthways, into small narrow strips.

Tearing the newspaper for the papier-mâché

2 Next, make the papier-mâché pulp, for the relief details on the surface of the screen. Place the shredded paper in a large, heavy-bottomed saucepan, cover it with cold water, and leave it to stand for at least two days. This will soften the paper, and break down the fibres.

3 While the paper is softening, paint the backs and edges of the panels with pale blue emulsion. Once the paint is completely dry, you may find this undercoat has raised the grain of the MDF. If so, sand the paint down with a fine grade sandpaper; this will remove any roughness, and give the surfaces a silky smooth feel.

4 Once the paper has soaked, place the saucepan on the cooker hob or ring, and bring the water to the boil. Simmer for at least one hour, then remove the saucepan from the heat, and mash the resulting pulp with an old potato masher, to break down the fibres.

Pushing the pulp through a sieve

5 Next, remove the excess water from the pulp. Tip the pulp into a sieve, a bit at a time, and press it down with a wooden spoon, to squeeze out the water.

6 Transfer the dry pulp to a clean and dry container (the saucepan, if you like), and sprinkle in a heaped tablespoon of dry wallpaper paste mix. Mix in the paste very thoroughly, to avoid lumps forming in the pulp.

Mixing the pulp with the paste

7 Once the paste and pulp have been thoroughly mixed, you can apply the pulp to the twining plant design on the front surfaces of the panels. The raised design should be about 6mm (¹/4in) thick, so only press small amounts of pulp onto the design at one time, using an old kitchen knife to build up the shapes so that they are smooth, well-defined and crisp. Continue in this way over the whole of each panel, until all the patterns are covered, then leave the panels to dry thoroughly.

Applying the pulp to the panel

8 It will take some time, possibly even some days, before the pulp is properly dry, so be patient. Because of the excess moisture in the pulp, the panels will have a tendency to warp; to counteract this, lay them flat on their backs, with weights placed at each end, until they are completely dry.

The copper paint has a cellulose base, which is not soluble in turpentine or water. If you don't have the cleaning solvent recommended by the manufacturer, apply the paint with an old paintbrush – you can then throw the brush away, if you are not able to clean it.

9 When the panels are dry, you can begin to decorate them. First, apply an undercoat of copper paint over the whole of the front of each panel, including the papier-mâché areas. Leave the paint to dry overnight, in a well-ventilated space.

Painting the copper undercoat

10 Once the copper paint is completely dry, you can begin to apply the verdigris effect to the fronts of the panels. Start with the papier-mâché details; these are painted with a darker colour, so they stand out from the background. Mix a small amount of both shades of acrylic paint together and, using a medium artists' brush, carefully paint over all the papier-mâché details, taking care to keep the edges neat. Leave to dry before continuing with the verdigris background.

Painting the papier-mâché details with acrylic

11 To achieve a good base of colour for the verdigris, you need to build up layers of paint. First, stipple green emulsion all over the surface of both the copper and the relief areas. To achieve the desired effect, some of the copper areas must still show through, so dab off any excess paint from the stippling brush before starting, to ensure the paint is not too thick; build up the density of colour gradually.

You can always add more colour later, if you need to. Don't worry if the result is patchy; this will add to the finished effect. When you have stippled the front of each panel, continue immediately with the next stage.

12 Next, apply a second coat of green emulsion over the stippled areas. This final coat should be very thin and watery, as it needs to simulate the streaks found on old bronze statues, that have been washed repeatedly by the rain.

Now water down a small amount of paint to a milky consistency, and stir well to remove any lumps. Stand each panel in an upright position, over many layers of newspaper to catch the drips, and begin to apply the paint.

13 Start at the top of the panel and, with the brush well loaded with paint, gently touch the panel surface with the brush, squeezing some of the paint out as you do so, so that it runs down the surface. Continue in this way, reloading the brush at intervals, until the panel is streaked with the paint, but remember, some of the previous coats of paint must still show through to achieve the correct effect.

Dripping on the top coat of emulsion

Liquid bronze leaf comes in a small bottle and, on standing, separates out, so mix it well before use, to distribute the metallic particles evenly throughout the base. The brush can be cleaned after use with turpentine.

14 If you need to make the runs and drips slightly less harsh, dip the paintbrush in a little clean water at intervals, and allow the water to run over the streaks, washing them and softening them a little. Only do this where necessary, though, otherwise you'll find that you have washed away all the paint that you have just applied. When you are satisfied with the results, leave the panels to dry overnight.

15 If you wish to sharpen up the relief areas, now is the time to reapply some of the acrylic paint mixture used in stage 10. Allow the paint to dry before going on to the final stage.

16 As a finishing touch, bronze liquid leaf is painted over the papier-mâché details, using a fine artists' brush. Carefully outline the edge of each papier-mâché area, and other details, such as the veins on the leaves. You might also like to add some further detail to the background, e.g. swirls in the corner of each panel, and along the edges at intervals. When you are happy with the decoration on each panel, leave the paint to dry overnight.

Highlighting the papier-mâché with liquid leaf

17 Once the liquid leaf is dry, seal the back, front and side of each panel with two coats of acrylic satin varnish, to prevent the leaf from tarnishing. Make sure the first coat of varnish is completely dry before applying the second coat.

18 You can now reattach the hinges (see detailed instructions on page 35) and your screen is complete.

MOROCCAN SCREEN
with mosaic decoration

Allow at least 1 week to complete

With this exotic and colourful screen, its panels bordered in fragments of brightly coloured tiles, I've aimed to capture the beauty and spirit of Morocco, where mosaic tiling plays a significant role, both in architecture and surface decoration. There, small pieces of vividly coloured tiles are used to create beautiful, intricately interwoven patterns for walls, floors and even ceilings.

My screen re-creates the feel and texture of the Moroccan style with broken household tiles. Because the tiles add quite a lot of weight to each panel, I have restricted them to a border of four rows, and have also cut out areas of the panels to reduce the overall weight of the screen. The centre 'tiles' are in fact printed, in colours to complement the mosaic tiling, and then highlighted with imitation silver leaf, which gives an extra shine and glitter to their surface.

If you would prefer to make a simpler, lighter screen, you could use a screen blank, and it would still be possible to create the same style of screen without the cut-out areas, and using fewer tiles – say two rows of tiles, instead of four.

MATERIALS AND EQUIPMENT

PREPARED PANELS, WITH MARKED-OUT DESIGN (SEE TEMPLATE ON PAGE 116), OR SCREEN BLANK (SEE PAGE 2)

BRIGHT BLUE SATIN EMULSION PAINT

MASKING TAPE

MEDIUM AND FINE GRADE SANDPAPER

ASSORTMENT OF PLAIN AND PATTERNED HOUSEHOLD TILES IN AT LEAST TWO COLOURS TO MATCH YOUR PAINT

TILE ADHESIVE

TILE GROUT

GLUE SPREADER (OPTIONAL, FOR USE WITH GROUT)

READY-MIXED BRIGHT BLUE POSTER OR ACRYLIC PAINT FOR TINTING THE GROUT (SEE 'NOTE' ON PAGE 93)

EMULSION PAINT IN VARYING COLOURS FOR 'FAKE' TILES. MATCH POTS OR PAINT REMNANTS ARE IDEAL (I USED YELLOW, RED, PALE BLUE AND PALE GREEN)

TILE PLIERS OR HAMMER (SEE PAGE 92)

SAFETY GOGGLES (ESSENTIAL)

GLOVES, FOR PROTECTION WHEN HANDLING TILES (COULD BE RUBBER GLOVES OR GARDENING GLOVES) (not shown in photographs)

3 OR 4 ORDINARY HOUSEHOLD FOAM SCOURERS

SHARP SCISSORS

IMITATION SILVER LEAF

SIZE TO STICK THE SILVER LEAF TO THE SURFACE

SMALL ARTISTS' BRUSH

SATIN ACRYLIC VARNISH

METHOD

1 First of all, paint in the background colour on the central, marked-out area of each panel, using the blue emulsion. This will form the base coat for printing the imitation tiles. You can, if you like, mark off the area with masking tape, to ensure a neater finish. Once the front is dry, paint the backs and edges of all three panels with the same paint, then leave the panels to dry completely.

Painting the middle of the panel

2 If you find this undercoat has raised the grain of the MDF slightly, making it rough to the touch, sand back the paint, first with the medium grade sandpaper and then with the fine grade. Continue sanding until all the areas are smooth to the touch, including the edges, which may need special attention. If you like the 'distressed' look of the sanded paint, leave it as it is. Otherwise, apply a top coat of the same paint to the back and sides, and leave to dry as before.

3 Next, cut the foam scourers into 2.5cm (1in) squares, to use as printing blocks for the 'fake' tiles. If you find the pieces are not perfectly square, or you need to cut smaller squares for the more intricate areas later, they can be trimmed with the scissors.

Sponging on the imitation tiles

Cutting the foam scourers

4 Before printing the tiles, stand the panels upright, with the marked designs facing forwards. This will make it easier to judge if the printed lines are straight. Select a paint colour for the outside border, and place a small amount on a paper plate or similar container. You can now print your first row of imitation tiles.

5 Hold the scouring edge of one of your 'printing blocks', and dip the foam side into the paint, until it is completely covered with paint. Dab off any excess paint on kitchen paper, to ensure your printed square has a clean edge.

Start at the bottom left-hand corner of the painted central section of the panel, and work up the side of the central area, using the painted edge as a guide. Remember to leave a slight gap between each printed tile, as this blue area around each one is the imitation tile grout. Reload your printing block frequently, to ensure the colour of the 'tiles' is consistent.

6 Continue printing one row around the whole of the central area with the first colour, until you are finally back where you began. Then, wash out your printing block with water, dry it thoroughly on kitchen paper and, with your next colour, go around the central area, on the inside of the first row.

Continue with all the other colours until the whole of the central section is covered in printed squares. You may have to repeat several colours to fill in the whole area.

Treat the other two panels in the same way, and leave the paint to dry completely before continuing with the next stage.

If you have an awkward area, where a printed 'square' won't fit, you can cut the block into smaller or irregular shapes to fill the gap.

---

7 Once the imitation tiling is dry, you can begin to tile the outside border, using the broken household tiles. There are two ways of breaking the tiles, depending on the effect that you wish to achieve. For this particular screen, I broke the tiles into fairly uniform squares, using the tile pliers. But, if you prefer more random shapes, you can break the tiles with a hammer (see stage 8).

First put on your safety goggles, then place the pliers approximately 2.5cm (1in) in from the edge of the tile and squeeze until the tile breaks. It should break into one long thin piece, which can then be broken in the same way along its length, into smaller pieces.

Try and keep the size of the squares equal, and discard any odd shaped or pointed pieces, so that the finished panel has a nice uniform effect.

Continue breaking the tiles in this way until you have sufficient small tile squares.

Breaking tiles with pliers

NOTE: safety goggles must be worn when breaking tiles, to protect your eyes from flying tile chips.

8 If you want more random shapes, break the tiles with a hammer, instead. Put on protective goggles, then place the tiles face down between the layers of an old blanket, to stop the chips flying. Hit the tiles firmly with the hammer, to break them into smaller pieces – it may take several blows before you have pieces small enough to use. Shards of broken tile are liable to become lodged underneath during smashing, so beware of damaging the surface glaze when breaking up the smaller pieces.

Breaking tiles with a hammer

9 Before sticking the tiles on the panel, mask off the adjacent area of the printed surface with masking tape; this will prevent it being spoilt by tile adhesive spreading over on to it and, when the tape is removed, it will ensure a clean edge.

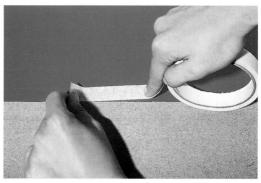

Masking off the blue central area with tape

10 When you have enough tiles for the borders of one panel, lay them out, so you can arrange them in a suitable pattern. I simply placed the tiles in four rows of matching colours, to completely fill the border area.

If you have broken your tiles more randomly, it may take longer to achieve a cohesive pattern. Arrange small sections of the design at a time, so you can see how the tiles will fit together before sticking them down with tile adhesive.

If adhesive squeezes out as you apply the tiles, remove the excess as you go along. This is easier than removing dried adhesive later, and also ensures that the pieces fit fairly closely together.

11 To stick the tiles to the panel, apply a small amount of tile adhesive to the back of each piece; this is neater and easier than trying to spread large areas of adhesive onto the panel itself, and enables you to control where the adhesive is placed. Press each separate tile into position, remembering to leave small gaps around each piece to accommodate the tile grout. Once one section is complete, move on to the next. Complete the tiled areas of each panel, then leave the panels to dry completely before grouting.

Sticking the broken tiles

NOTE: poster paint is best for tinting the amount of grout needed here, but it won't give a great depth of colour, as the grout is liable to become runny if too much of the paint is added.

If you want a deep colour, you could use artists' acrylic paint straight from the tube. Acrylic paint is less liquid, and also has a higher density of pigment to give a deeper colour, but is more expensive, so best used only for small amounts.

12 You may like to use a coloured grout, as I have done here, as it is less stark than plain white grout and makes the finished tiling look a little more authentic. You can buy coloured grout at most large DIY stores, but you can just as easily make your own using ordinary white tile grout, tinted with poster or acrylic paint (see 'Note' above). Whichever you choose, add some of the paint to the tile grout and mix well to achieve the colour of your choice. You are then ready to begin grouting.

Colouring the grout

13 To grout the tiles, use the applicator provided with your adhesive or grout or, for more intricate areas, use a glue spreader. With the flattest side, press the grout into the gaps, smoothing it across as you go. Continue over the entire area until each space is completely filled with the grout and the surface is fairly level. Leave the grout to set for a few minutes, but do not let it dry out completely before beginning to clean off the excess.

Applying the grout

14 Remove any excess grout from the surface of the tiles using a large flat sponge (or another of your foam scourers) dipped in clean warm water, then squeezed out. It is important to remove most of the water from the sponge, and to keep the sponge flat against the tiles as you wipe, otherwise you risk pulling out the grout from between the tiles as well.

It may take several attempts to clean the tiles completely, so rinse your sponge regularly to prevent it becoming clogged with grout, or you will smear it back over the surface.

When you have cleaned all the tiles in this way, leave them to dry thoroughly before polishing off any dusty areas with a soft cloth.

Repeat the process on the other two panels.

Cleaning off the grout

It is best to size small areas at a time until you have a better idea of how the finished panel will look. You can always keep adding to the leafed areas until you are satisfied with the results.

15 Once the mosaic tiles are clean, you can highlight the imitation tiles with silver leaf. First, apply size to the areas where you want the silver leaf. The size acts as a glue for the thin silver sheets, and can be applied most accurately using a small artists' brush. Don't apply size to all the imitation tiles, but pick out areas randomly, so that silver highlights are distributed over the entire painted area of the panel. You can cover whole tiles or just parts of tiles but, once the size has been applied, it must be left at least 15 minutes to dry before attaching the silver leaf. Once the size is ready, it changes colour from milky-white to clear and feels tacky to the touch.

Applying the size for the silver leaf

16 When the size is ready, take a sheet of silver leaf, with its backing still intact, and lay it silver-side-down on a sized area. Then, using a soft paintbrush, smooth over the backing paper to adhere the leaf to the size.

Applying the silver leaf

When you have fixed one area, carefully peel off the backing paper, and use a soft cloth (or kitchen paper) to gently polish the surface of the leaf and remove any excess flakes. These flakes can be used again if sufficiently large but, if they are very small, discard them.

Rubbing off the excess leaf

Continue in the same way until all the sized areas have been covered with the silver leaf.

17 When you have tiled and leafed all your panels, you must varnish the imitation tile area in the centre of each one. This is to protect the paint from wear, as well as to protect the silver leaf from tarnishing.

Apply two coats of acrylic varnish, leaving time in between for the first coat to dry thoroughly.

Once the second coat of varnish is dry, you can attach the hinges to the panels and complete your screen (see detailed instructions on page 35).

Varnishing the panels

ROMAN-STYLE SCREEN

with mosaics and faux marbling

Mosaic and marble were used extensively in Roman times, for both the exteriors and interiors of buildings. This screen, with its faux marble central panel and decorative mosaic details, is based on the kind of designs the Romans might have used, as well as introducing some of the tones and colours that were – and still are – prevalent in the Mediterranean region. The resulting screen is richly textured and elaborately decorated, using gold paint, mosaic tiles and marbling techniques that, with a little practice, can easily be re-created by the complete amateur at home.

If you prefer, you could simplify the process by using 'shmalti' – small tile chippings, available from specialist outlets – instead of breaking up household tiles.

MATERIALS AND EQUIPMENT

SHAPED PANELS, WITH PRE-MARKED DESIGN (SEE TEMPLATE ON PAGE 117) OR SCREEN BLANK (SEE PAGE 2)

BRILLIANT WHITE SATIN EMULSION PAINT

MEDIUM AND FINE GRADE SANDPAPER

ACRYLIC VARNISH

ACRYLIC SCUMBLE GLAZE

ARTISTS' ACRYLIC PAINT: YELLOW OCHRE, RAW SIENNA, BURNT UMBER, WHITE, BLACK

ARTISTS' BRUSHES, BOTH FINE AND MEDIUM

SOFTENING BRUSH

HOUSEHOLD TILES FOR THE MOSAIC, OR 'SHMALTI' (SEE PREVIOUS PAGE)

SAFETY GOGGLES, PROTECTIVE GLOVES AND TILE PLIERS (IF HOUSEHOLD TILES ARE USED)

LOW-TACK MASKING TAPE

TILE ADHESIVE AND GROUT

GLUE STICK OR SPREADER

LIME-FREE GRAVEL OR SMALL PEBBLES (TO ADD TEXTURE AND VARIATION)

GOLD POSTER PAINT

COBALT BLUE POSTER PAINT

FLAT-ENDED ARTISTS' BRUSH

NOTE: if you use lime-free gravel, make sure it has been washed thoroughly before use, to remove any traces of dirt or sand.

METHOD

1 First, paint the central marked area of all three panels with the white emulsion. This is the undercoat for the faux marbling. Leave the panels to dry overnight, or as directed on the tin.

Undercoating the central marked area of the panel

2 Once the paint is dry, you may find the paint has raised the grain of the wood, making it rough to the touch. If so, sand back the panels with the medium grade and then the fine grade sandpaper, until you have a nice smooth surface on which to apply the next coat of paint.

3 Now apply a second coat of white emulsion to the same area of each panel, and leave to dry as before. Sand back again, to give a flatter paint colour.

4 The centre of the panels must have a fairly shiny surface, so that the paint for the marbled effect can be pushed and spread over it, so the next step is to paint the white emulsioned areas with two coats of satin acrylic varnish. Allow the first coat of varnish to dry for at least four hours before applying the second coat, then leave all three panels to dry overnight.

Varnishing the centre of a panel

5 When the varnish is completely dry, you may begin the marbling.

First, mix equal parts of yellow ochre acrylic paint and white acrylic paint (approx. one teaspoon of each). Then add half a teaspoon of burnt umber, to achieve a light coloured beige. You will need approximately two parts of white and yellow ochre paint to one part of burnt umber. Next, in a separate container, mix equal parts of white and burnt umber to obtain a darker brownish beige.

To each of these colours add roughly equal measures of acrylic scumble glaze and mix thoroughly. The scumble glaze should make the paint more transparent, and easier to move around the surface when it's applied to the panel. If the paint and scumble mixture still seem a little thick, add more of the scumble glaze until the paint has a fairly runny, creamy consistency. It's then ready to apply.

Applying acrylic paint and scumble glaze

When painting the faux marble, don't try to work on the whole panel at once, only do small areas at a time; this will prevent the paint drying out before the next stage. Do the top section of each panel first, then the middle, then the bottom, blending each section together as you go.

6 First, lay the screen panels in a horizontal position. You can then start to paint in the base coat of faux marbling, with the medium-sized artists' brush.

Start from the top left hand corner of the emulsioned area, and apply diagonal lines of paint, alternating between the two mixed colours, until you achieve the desired effect. Do not cover the entire white surface with the paint, but leave gaps so that the white background shows through.

It's a good idea to practise painting the faux marble effect on an offcut of MDF before you start on the actual panels.

7 Now, create the marble effect, by softening and blending the scumble mixtures together with the softening brush.

Start in the top left-hand corner of the panel and brush briskly back and forth, diagonally, i.e. along the lines of the scumble paint, and in the direction of the marble grain. Keep your wrist loose to achieve flowing strokes along the paint, and brush out the paint until one colour is blended into another and the entire area is covered in paint. Repeat the process on the other two panels, then leave them to dry overnight.

'Softening' with the brush

NOTE: if you find that the surface is not covered adequately, quickly fill in the gaps, but bear in mind that you can only re-apply once; if you continue brushing over the same area, you will begin to create deep brush marks on the surface instead of achieving a smooth effect.

After brushing out each section, wash and dry your softening brush thoroughly to remove any traces of paint. If the bristles are clogged, it will prevent the paint drying and ultimately affect the smoothness of the finish on other areas.

NOTE: the panels must be completely dry before the veins are added otherwise, when 'softening' the veins, the first coat will lift and smudge and spoil the effect.

8 Once the base coat of the marbling has been completed, prepare the paint for the veins.

Mix a small amount of black artists' acrylic paint with some of the scumble glaze, roughly two parts of paint to one part glaze. Then, separately mix the same proportions of glaze with black and white acrylic to form a mid-grey colour, and with white paint for the highlight veins.

9 Add the dark veins first, using a fine artists' paintbrush; aim for very fine veins that radiate across diagonally, along the grain of the previous undercoat marbling.

Load up the paintbrush with the black paint and, beginning in the top left-hand corner of the panel, drag the brush along the surface, rotating it as you go, and wiggling it slightly to form a fairly uneven line. Try not to deviate too far from a linear progression, but do not have the line too even, either – break the line in places to more realistically mimic the look of real marble.

Painting on the dark veins

10 Next, highlight some areas of the black lines with the mid-grey paint. There is no need to wash the brush between colours as the two colours should merge together.

NOTE: do not try to cover the whole area of the panel with the veins before 'softening', as you may find that the initial areas have dried too much and will therefore not 'soften' with the brush.

11 Continue adding the black lines to each section of the panel. Paint a few at a time over each area, 'softening' as you go, by brushing briskly back and forth with the softening brush to 'smudge' the paint.

If you would like a more feathered effect in a few isolated areas, brush a little more in a side-to-side direction to spread the paint out across the vein.

When you are satisfied with one area, clean the softening brush to prevent the paint drying on the bristles, and continue in the same way until the whole of each panel is covered.

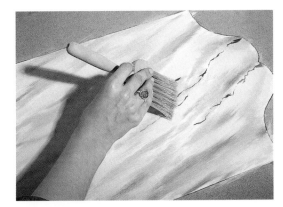

Softening the veins

Faux marbling detail

12 Now you can add white highlight veins, to give the surface more texture.

Apply the white paint mixture in the same way as you applied the dark veins; place each white vein between the darker ones, and take care to maintain a diagonal pattern. Soften the veins as before, then repeat the whole process on the other two panels.

Leave the panels to dry overnight.

Painting on light veins

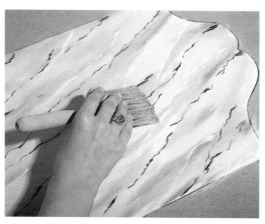

Softening the light veins

13 Next day, seal the marbled areas of the panels with a coat of satin acrylic varnish. Allow the varnish to dry thoroughly, then apply a second coat.

Varnishing the faux marble

14 Once the marbling is complete, and the varnish dry, you can tile the outside border using broken household tiles or 'shmalti'.

CAUTION: REMEMBER THAT SAFETY GOGGLES MUST BE WORN WHEN BREAKING TILES, TO PROTECT YOUR EYES FROM FLYING SHARDS.

To break the tiles, place the tile pliers about 2.5cm (1in) in from the edge of the tile, and squeeze until it breaks. It should break into one long thin piece, which can then be broken in the same away along its length, into smaller pieces. Try and keep the size of the squares equal, and discard any odd shaped or pointed pieces so that the finished panel has a nice uniform effect. Continue breaking the tiles in this way until you have sufficient small tile squares for your border.

15 Lay out the whole of your design before fixing the pieces, to ensure that you have enough tiles and that you like the design.

Before sticking the tiles on the panels, place masking tape along the adjacent edges of the faux marbling. This will prevent tile adhesive spreading onto the painted area, and ensure a nice clean edge when the tape is remove.

Next, place your broken tiles or 'shmalti' along the lines traced on the panels, remembering to leave a gap around each one for the grout.

16 To stick the tiles in position, spread a small amount of adhesive on the back of each mosaic piece as you go; this is neater and easier than trying to spread large areas of adhesive on the panel itself, and gives you more control over the placing of the adhesive.

Position the tiles, remembering the gap all around each one for the grout, and press down well to ensure the tiles are stuck firmly to the surface.

Continue sticking down all your tiles in this way, then leave the three panels to dry overnight.

Masking off marbled area before tiling

Applying the tiles

If adhesive squeezes out from underneath a tile as you stick it down, remove the excess as you go along. This is easier than removing dried adhesive later, and also ensures that the pieces fit fairly closely together.

17 Once the tiles are stuck down firmly, prepare some coloured grouting by combining a small amount of burnt umber artists' acrylic paint with white grout. Mix both together thoroughly until you achieve the desired colour, then press the adhesive into the spaces between the tiles, using the glue stick or spreader. Remember to cover the exposed tile edges with the grout, to obtain a neat finish.

Colouring the grout

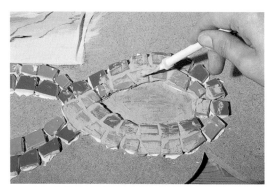

Applying the grout

18 Once all the spaces between the tiles have been filled, allow the grout to solidify slightly, then clean off any excess grout and adhesive with a damp sponge soaked in warm water. Don't try to do this too soon, or you may pull the grout out of the spaces with the sponge.

19 Next, add gravel to the gaps in the centre of the mosaic designs, for texture and variation. First fill the gaps in with coloured grout, then push in the gravel pieces. Once you have filled these areas, you can fill in other random areas around the tiles in the same way, to give a more uneven look. Once this is completed, leave the gravel areas to dry overnight.

Adding the gravel

20 After tiling, there may be areas of the panel which still show the plain MDF. To cover these areas, apply a rough coat of the tile grout with the spreader, to obtain a plastered effect. Leave the grout to dry as before.

Applying a rough coat of grout

21 When the basic tiling and gravelling are complete, you can add a finishing touch by applying a row of tiles around the border of the marbled area.

First, remove the line of masking tape carefully, making sure that you don't pull off any of the paint beneath it. Then lay out a row of tiles as before; stick and grout them as previously, making doubly sure that none of the grout or adhesive sticks to the marbled area.

22 Once all the tiling is finished, you can add a little extra shine by painting over random areas of grouting and gravel, using a dry brush with the antique gold poster paint. Dip the brush into the paint, dab off the excess on kitchen paper, then rub the surface of the gravel with the brush. This technique should transfer the paint only very sparsely, highlighting the raised areas. If you like, you can add extra interest by repeating this process using the blue poster paint.

23 When the painting is complete, clean away any excess that has been brushed onto the tiles. Finish the edges of each panel with gilding cream (or the same gold paint), and when dry, seal all painted areas (including the gravel) with one coat of acrylic varnish. You can now reattach the hinges (see detailed instructions on page 35) and your screen is complete.

Applying gilding cream to the edges

Highlighting with gold poster paint

Varnishing the gravel

TEMPLATES
for solid panel screens

N.B. If you have decided to make a solid panel screen, you will need to transfer your chosen design from the template to a paper pattern. Detailed instructions for this are given on page 31, under 'Making a paper pattern'.

Country-look Screen

(see page 37)

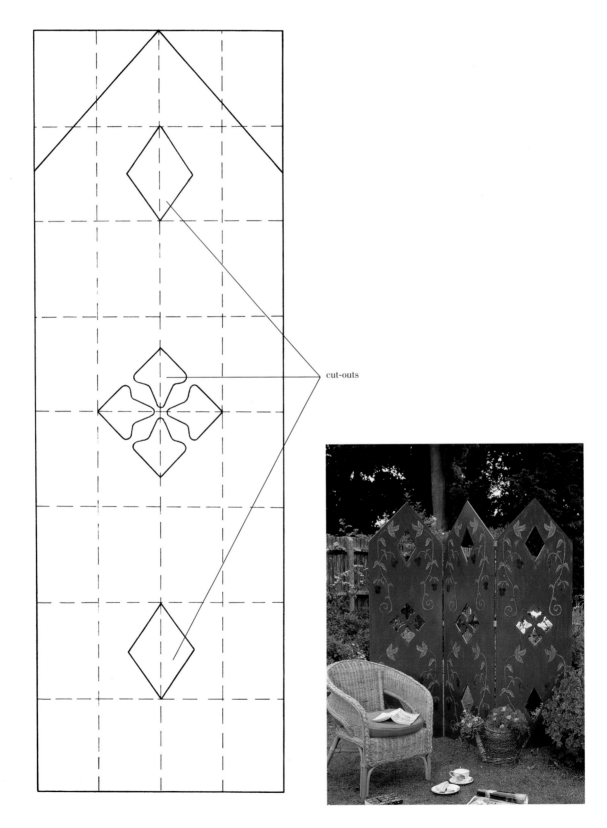

cut-outs

Leather-effect Screen

(see page 43)

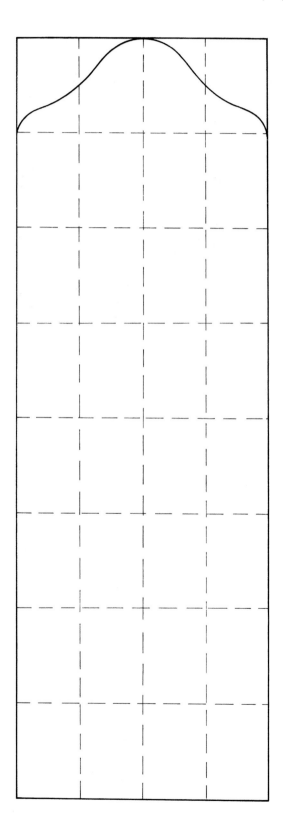

Upholstered Screen

(see page 49)

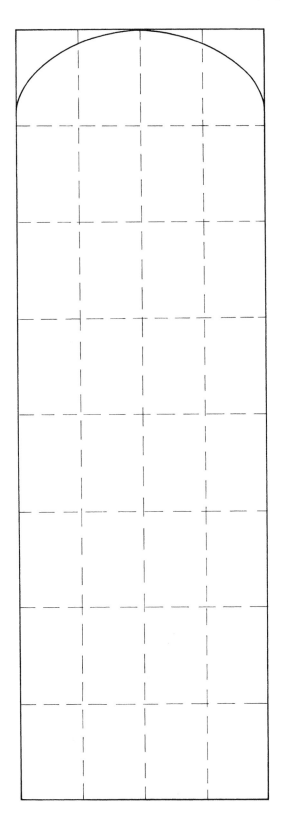

Driftwood Screen

(see page 55)

MIDDLE PANEL

SIDE PANEL

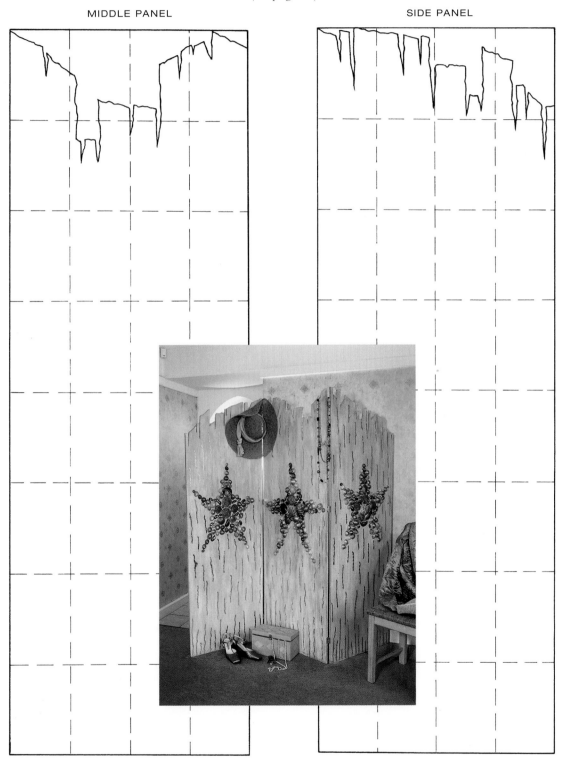

N.B. Remember the side panels are mirror images.
Reverse this template for the left panel.

Music Score Screen

(see page 61)

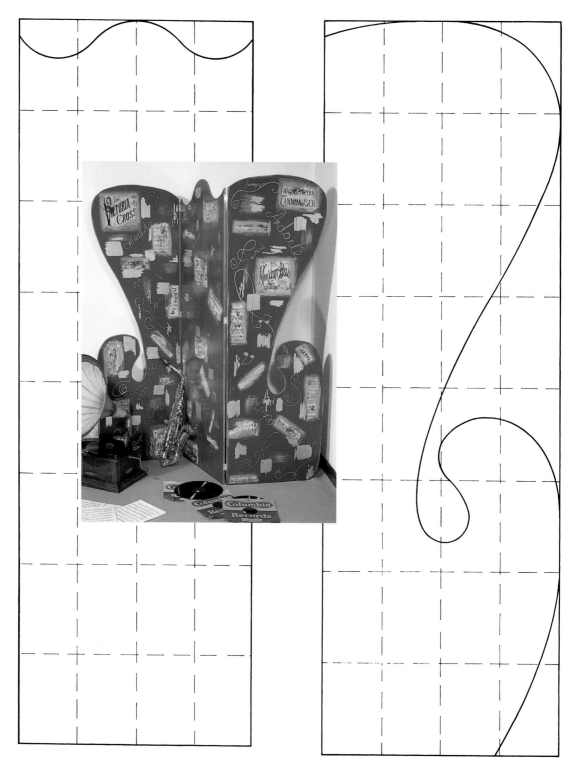

N.B. Remember the side panels are mirror images.
Reverse this template for the left panel.

Decoupage Screen

(see page 69)

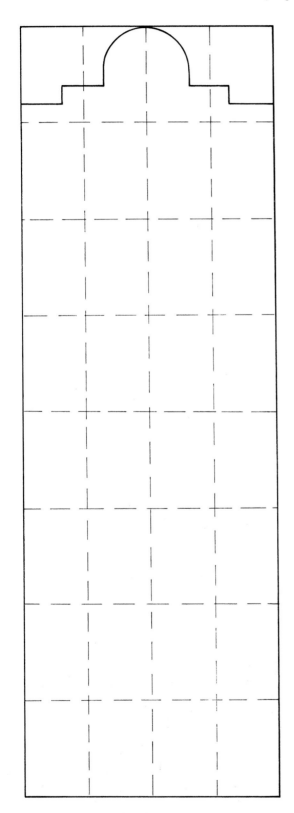

Wallpapered Screen

(see page 75)

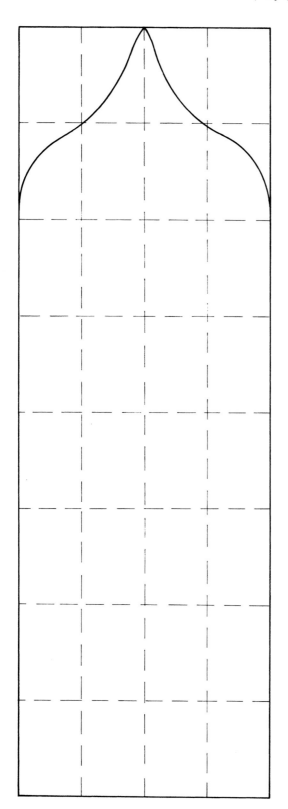

Verdigris Screen

(see page 83)

Moroccan Screen

(see page 89)

cut-out

mosaic tiles

'fake' tile effect